OPERATION BAD APPLE

G.F. NEWMAN

The Royal Court Writers Series
published by Methuen
in association with the Royal Court Theatre

All characters, names, crimes and incidents contained in this play have been invented. Any similarities to persons living or dead are coincidental. Offices have been named solely for the sake of locale and the play is in no way intended to reflect attitudes or opinions of those persons holding such offices past or present.

First published in 1982 by Methuen London Ltd, 11 New Fetter Lane, London EC4P 4EE in association with the Royal Court Theatre, Sloane Square, London SW1.
Reprinted 1982

ISBN 0 413 50270 8

Operation Bad Apple was first performed at the Royal Court Theatre, London, on 4 February 1982, with the following cast:

ASSISTANT COMMISSIONER (AC) PETER VYVYAN
DR ROALD BOSÉ
} Richard Wilson

DETECTIVE CHIEF INSPECTOR TERRY SNEED   Patrick Malahide

DRIVER
DETECTIVE CHIEF SUPERINTENDENT
   TONY BULMER
BAR MANAGER
ATTORNEY GENERAL SIR WALTER PURSAR
} Nigel Terry

DETECTIVE SERGEANT DEL PREECE
COMMANDER ERNIE WISEMAN
} Roger Booth

DETECTIVE CONSTABLE ROY HORN
ASSISTANT CHIEF CONSTABLE ALAN LEEPER
BRIAN CAYMAN
} Richard Ireson

DETECTIVE SERGEANT LENNY FEAST
COMMISSIONER SIR DENIS WHITES
GAOLER
} Colin McCormack

DETECTIVE CHIEF INSPECTOR BRIAN HUMPFRESS
DIRECTOR OF PUBLIC PROSECUTIONS
   SIR TREVOR RUMP
} Toby Salaman

Directed by Max Stafford-Clark
Designed by Peter Hartwell

'If it's on the table,
eat it.'

Prologue

'For those of you who don't know me, I am Assistant Commissioner Vyvyan,' *the senior Met Officer says to the large gathering of detectives before him. He is Assistant Commissioner Peter Vyvyan, who's a thin, fifty-one-year-old, wearing an expensive, well-cut suit.* 'You all know why you're here, so I don't propose going over ground that will be covered by your individual squad briefing officers. Other than to say you will probably never have a more important investigation to conduct for its far-reaching consequences; never have a more difficult investigation, nor one where you'll get so little thanks if you prove successful. But I know you won't allow that to influence you. You are all very experienced detectives, and highly thought of by your commanding officers, if you weren't you wouldn't have been told to volunteer. You are not Met officers, a fact that has been made much of in the press and on television. So let me set the record straight here and now. There is nothing sinister about having an outside force investigate the possible wrong-doing in the Met, despite the neurotic criticism that this is simply more police looking at police. Of course it's one lot of policemen investigating another. It's a matter of historical fact that there is no outside body capable of conducting such investigations as efficiently as the police. Also a matter of historical fact here in the Met we have always welcomed impartial and objective investigation of complaints. That's the only way we can be assured of keeping our good name.

'Your brief is to leave no complaint against the police uninvestigated, no matter how trivial or insignificant. And a lot of the complaints will be just that, and worse, down-right malicious – villains trying to settle old scores against policemen who proved unbending. I'm confident that at the end of your inquiry, however long it takes, the reputations of the majority of Met officers will be fully restored. What we're in fact talking about here is the odd bad apple in an otherwise sound barrel. But this is no excuse for complacency. We're realistic enough to know the odd bad apple does exist, so let us dig it out. We don't need to tolerate bent coppers, and nor will we, because like me, most decent, hard-working policemen prize the reputation they've worked so hard to earn. But I'll say no more about that as I have no wish to preempt your conclusions.

'The hour is late,' *he says, glancing at his watch,* 'and most of you have been working full stretch down in Wiltshire to clear your own jobs. So I won't delay you unnecessarily. As from now the Met is on trial, the media ne'er-do-wells and those who are politically motivated expect you to find every one of us guilty; having done so they'll then expect us to provide the whitewash. So whatever the outcome we can't win. However, both the commissioner and the home secretary have given their personal assurances that there won't be any white wash. Both the director of public prosecutions and the attorney general will make absolutely certain there isn't. The results of your investigation will be acted upon swiftly and decisively.

'Your task won't be made easier by virtue of your being strangers to London. I don't doubt the last time you were up here was when Swindon was playing in the FA cup final. Traditionally when a detective takes his investigation to another policeman's manor he is given local assistance. Here you will get no help from the Met, except in the use of drivers and police stations. What you can expect, and will get, is the fullest cooperation whenever you wish to interview police officers. But remember, just because you'll be dealing with policemen, that doesn't mean you should pull your punches.

'Well, good luck!'

AC Peter Vyvyan leaves the rostrum.

Darkness.

ACT ONE

One

Peter Vyvyan, in shirtsleeves and a summer hat is snoozing, propped up on a sunbed in the garden of his house in Esher. He doesn't stir when a man in his mid-thirties comes into the garden. The visitor is wearing a decent suit and a tie and is carrying a briefcase. He is Detective Chief Inspector Terry Sneed. He waits a moment, then switches off the horse racing on the portable TV, which has a wire from the house.

'Guv', *Sneed says, as the man starts awake.*

'Oh, hello there . . . chief inspector,' *Peter Vyvyan says as if not certain how to address the man.* 'I was just watching the racing,' *he apologises as he sits up, convinced he wasn't asleep.*

'When Mrs Vyvyan said you were in the garden, I thought she meant you were doing a bit,' *Sneed says.*

'I have three days well-earned leave,' *AC Vyvyan says.* 'Gardening's not my idea of relaxation. That's her department. Is she making some tea?'

'I didn't ask,' *Sneed replies. There is a slight awkwardness to their conversation at first, it's more than just simply uncertainty over how to address one another, there being a big difference in rank. It's almost as if they'd rather this familiar meeting wasn't taking place.*

'I expect she will,' *Vyvyan says.* 'Have you just come from the Yard?'

'I made one or two calls on the way down,' *Sneed tells him.*

'I thought you were a bit later than you said. It made me wonder.'

'I was going to give you a bell,' *Sneed says.* 'But I thought it best to give the telephone a miss.'

'You don't think the Turnip Squad are contemplating tapping my phone, Terry, do you?' *AC Vyvyan asks in slight alarm.*

'Well they've had a go at just about everyone else.'

'Yes,' *the AC says.* 'No stone, as they say.'

'They're mostly charging around like blue-arsed flies, they're investigating irrelevant tittle-tattle.'

'They didn't agree when I pointed that out at one of our meetings,' *the AC says.*

'If they have got a line on *your* phone I wouldn't fancy anyone else's chances. I was just being cautious, 'is all.'

'That's no bad thing,' *Peter Vyvyan says.* 'Some policemen were not only getting very greedy, but very careless also. Greed I can tolerate, just – I'm a firm believer in the Government's monetarist policy, letting the market find it's own price – what is unforgivable is carelessness. There was no need for it. How much did you bring me this month?'

'Ten per cent comes to £3,894,' *DCI Sneed tells him.*

'That's a bit light,' *the AC says.*

'It reflects what Bad Apple is doing to business, guv,' *Sneed tells him.* 'Everyone's being double careful.'

'Yes, but I thought the price was going up as a result. You might have rounded it up to an even £4,000. It's difficult enough to keep rounded figures straight in one's head,' *Vyvyan complains,* 'much less odd bits.'

'I daresay we can chip in the other sixteen sovs, guv, if it helps you out.'

'I appreciate that.' *He sits forward, slapping Sneed on the knee.* 'Good, that makes life a bit easier. I only wish the real headache caused by all this cash every month was solved as easily.'

'Well, I could give you a cheque, guv,' *Sneed jokes.*

'It's all right for you, Terry,' *the AC reflects,* 'a single man with the sort of income your rank gives you, you're permitted to live a little flamboyantly. I have to be so careful. What do villains do with their money, Terry?' *the AC says.* 'I always meant to ask.'

Sneed considers him a moment. 'They mostly splash it about and get themselves grassed. That's how they all come to be nicked.'

'Oh, I thought it was because you manufactured the evidence.'

'Some need of that.'

'We went to Venice for a holiday back in May,' *the AC confesses.* 'I thought we'd do it in style. We stayed at the Danieli, the very best hotel, right on the Riva degli Schiavoni. Bugger me if we didn't run into the DPP and his wife.'

'I expect he was doing the same thing, guv,' *Sneed says.* 'Getting rid of some loose change.'

'I'd like to think so. I don't know what your solution is, you've obviously found one.' *He waits a moment, as if expecting Sneed to tell him.* 'Oh well,' *he says, when Sneed doesn't,* 'I certainly find it a problem.'

AC Vyvyan notices the television is silent. 'What won the three-thirty at Sandown, did you notice?'

'Can't say I did,' *Sneed says.*

'You know what race that one was don't you?' *Vyvyan says.* 'That's the one where form goes haywire, and all the trainers who have had nothing but losers this season get their money back. All the smart money goes on the rank outsider.'

'Were you on?' *Sneed asks.*

'I never gamble,' *AC Vyvyan says piously.* 'If I had my way I'd have all those detectives from Wiltshire investigating *that* sort of corruption. You've heard what the latest move is? More detectives being brought onto Bad Apple.'

'That's cheering everyone up,' *Sneed says.* 'As if those already here aren't causing enough aggravation.'

'There was little I could do,' *AC Vyvyan apologises.* 'I did suggest the introduction of Met officers in order to push the investigation on to some conclusion. I don't have to tell you how that was received.'

'This is all ballocks!' *Sneed says on a flare of anger.* 'They're bringing more and more policemen onto Operation Bad Apple to interview more and more policemen. And for what? A big fat fuck all at the end of the day.'

'I sincerely hope you're right, Terry,' *AC Vyvyan says, looking slightly uneasy at the language this man has used.* 'Nothing causes quite the bad taste in my mouth as policemen being arrested.'

''Course I'm fucking right,' *Sneed says.* 'With the greatest respect, sir, I don't think you or the commissioner or anyone else at that level realises just what harm is being done by this investigation. A lot of good detectives getting thoroughly demoralised, a lot are putting in their papers. These are the men the service can't afford to lose.'

'I'm entirely sympathetic, Terry, and I know the commissioner feels the same way,' *Vyvyan says.* 'But you know where the pressure is coming from.'

'Well, I'm only a working detective,' *Sneed says.* 'But if you ask me I'd say this investigation has got to end, and soon. There's no deeply entrenched corruption here – even the Turnip Squad would have claimed more than a half dozen low ranking detectives after nine months. What's happened is, the villains we've had too many results with are making monkeys out of these country policemen. What's worse, the cunts are listening to them.'

Peter Vyvyan looks around a little concerned. 'Can you moderate your language a bit, Terry? This is Esher after all.'

'Oh, sorry, guv.' *Sneed says, simply lowering his voice.* 'But this is a terrible fucking situation we're getting into. No one wants to believe the policeman any more.'

'It's a very *dangerous* situation,' *Vyvyan says.* 'When the general public can no longer trust its policemen, that's going to be a very sorry day for the general public. That's why the home secretary is so concerned to restore public confidence.' *He says this as if it's their hard luck and not the fault of the police.*

'Well I'm not sure if this is the right way to go about it,' *Sneed tells him.*

'I'm afraid our betters tend not to be as sophisticated as you and I, Terry.' *Vyvyan concedes.* 'A more effective way of restoring confidence would be to follow my plan and drive the general public to a point of desperation through apparent lawlessness. Going for the most vulnerable flashpoint: racial tension. If we continue a policy of harassment of ethnic minorities, and bring about riot situations, with arson and looting, the home secretary will have a public outcry for stronger police measures. But whatever we do, if at the end of the day the general public is not reassured, then they're going to find some of the law and order proposals we're seeking a very bitter pill.'

'Well I'd say their only hope of pulling something out of the bag with this investigation is finding a deep throat with rank,' *Sneed comments.*

Vyvyan looks at him for a moment. 'Someone like you, Terry? I have bad dreams about that.'

'If only everyone was as careful as me, guv,' *Sneed says.*

'That's very reassuring.' *He looks towards the house.* 'I wonder what's happened to that tea. Vera must have popped over to India House for it.'

'I won't stop for tea,' *Sneed informs him, opening his briefcase.* 'I've got a couple of other calls to make.'

'Well come into the house, Terry,' *the AC says, rising.* 'I don't want the neighbours to see you handing me anything remotely resembling a parcel of money.'

They go inside.

Two

Detective Sergeant Del Preece, who's in his forties, overweight and ground down by a year away from home on 'Operation Bad Apple', is lounging in the back of a police car, his feet up over the front seat. Detective Constable Roy Horn, who's also in his forties, and thin, is in the other rear seat. A Met Driver is behind the wheel.

They wait; bored; tired.

The driver, who is partially in uniform, has a marked Cockney accent compared to the slight West Country burrs of the detectives. He looks at his watch. 'I wouldn't have thought much was going to happen again tonight, skip,' *he says.* 'Someone must've marked this villain's card.'

'Ah, could be a long night, at that,' *DS Preece concedes, settling himself.*

'I know a boozer up the road where we can get in the back door,' *the driver says.* 'I should think you could use a drink, the sort of month you've had. Ain't nicked fuck all, have you, apart from your throat shaving. Nor last month, did you.'

They look at him, but say nothing.

'Still, s'another mortgage payment gone,' *the driver says. He slides down making himself more comfortable.*

After a moment DS Preece says, 'Did your old woman have her chavvy yet, Roy?'

DC Horn sits up. 'How did you know she was knocked-up? She only went to the doctor this morning, man.'

'Months ago,' *DS Preece says.* 'You told me months ago, man.'

'She had that little fucker a year ago, near on,' *DC Horn says.* 'Just after we started on this lot.'

'Get on, it can't be that long. She's in the family way again?' *DS Preece says.* 'You're doing well.'

'I can't see I've had enough weekends home for it to be mine – she swears it is,' *DC Horn says solemnly.*

'This lot's not doing anyone's family life much good,' *DS Preece says.* 'No one dreamed it would go on this long. Why don't you ask for a transfer back home to normal duties?'

'I don't know as I wants to go back now,' *DC Horn says.*

'Here,' *the driver says, sitting up.* 'D'you hear about the Old Bill who caught two lovers bang to rights in the back of a car? He said, "All right, either it's my turn next or *you're* nicked." So he's waiting there at the car door, with a raving popcorn, after a couple of minutes the fella shoots his lot, then gets out of the car, trembling like a leaf. The officer says, "What's the matter with you, what you shaking for?" "I'm scared," the fella says, "I've never fucked a policeman before".'

It falls stone dead on the two detectives in the back.

After a moment DS Preece sits forward.

'Just who exactly is this officer?' *he asks.*

The driver looks at him, nonplussed. 'It's a joke,' *he explains.* 'S'fucking joke. What's the matter with you blokes? You're so fucking jumpy – what you need is a drink.' *He looks at his watch.* 'All right if I just slip down the road and have a shit, skip? I got a touch of diarrhoea.'

'Well, I suppose if you must,' *DS Preece says*. 'But don't be too long, case we get a shout.'

'The only shout you'll hear tonight is last orders from that pub,' *the driver says as he gets out of the car and goes*.

'I could use a drink myself,' *DC Horn says*.

DS Preece looks at his watch. 'There'll be god knows what to pay if we got a call on this lad.'

'The driver could be right,' *DC Horn says*. 'He often is.'

DS Del Preece yawns. This his colleague finds infectious. DC Horn yawns also. They are barely able to keep awake.

'Let's hope he's wrong this time,' *Preece says, looking at his watch*. 'I'm getting poxed off with this job.'

'This is the third fucking night on the spin we've been up,' *DC Horn complains, misunderstanding the DS*.

'The whole operation, being up in London, away from the family; away from the kind of villains you know.'

'I can't say that I'm bothered myself,' *DC Horn says*. 'There's plenty of fiddle on overtime and expenses.'

'I was going home at the weekend to buy a new car,' *DS Preece says*.

'What kind?' *DC Horn says*.

'A Mark IV Cortina,' *DS Preece says*. 'There's a dealer in Devizes, he's going to give me a nice discount.'

DC Horn looks at him with the obvious question.

'About 50% off the list price,' *DS Preece explains*. 'I overlooked a couple of things for him. It's a lovely motor. I didn't get to bed last weekend, much less get home.'

'Oh, yeah. Where d'you do that ol' WPC then?' *DC Horn asks with a smile*. 'Hump her against the station wall?'

'She couldn't contain herself long enough for bed,' *DS Preece says, enjoying the memory*.

'I'd sooner the ten quid whore I had in Compton Street,' *DC Horn says, remembering his wife's pregnancy*. 'I might as well.'

'You never gave one of that rubbish ten quid?' *Preece wants to know*.

'Did I fuck,' *DC Roy Horn says*. 'I shoved m' warrant card up her nose and told her I was investigating police corruption.'

'I know this, Roy,' *Preece says on a sombre note*, 'some of them know a lot more than we. That club owner we pinched the other week, he reckons most of the Porn Squad and Serious Crime Squad are taking money.'

'S'just rumours,' *Horn says*.

'I'm not so sure. No smoke without fire. Getting a free gobble's one thing, as my old gran used to say, there's no harm in that,' *Preece says*. 'That's not getting a living like a lot of these ponces in the Met.' *He pauses and looks cautiously about him*. 'You know whose name's come up more than once? Commander Wiseman. Be a brave policeman who pinches him.'

'It'll happen, Del,' *DC Horn says*, 'providing there's the evidence. There's got to be the evidence.'

'Can't see it happening, myself,' *DS Preece says*, 'not after this long. We got no one higher than a sergeant. I tell you, enough senior officer's names have been coughed for some sort of action. They're making fucking monkeys out of us.'

'You been up here too long, Del,' *DC Horn says*. 'That's your trouble. You're starting to *think* like a Met officer. Just because you got a suspect's name, you think it's enough. You can bend the rest. This'll do me for another year. I must have screwed more women than I knew existed in Wiltshire.'

'We need something to get this investigation out of the doldrums. Put us all on the train back home.'

The radio telephone crackles to life.

'You playing with your cocks back there or what?' *a disembodied voice says*. 'We've got a tickle. It's time to move in.'

'Our fucking driver's not here.' *DS Preece announces, as if realising for the first time*.

'What?' *the voice says*.

'He's gone for a shit,' *Preece explains*.

'You cunts!' *the voice says*. 'he's a Met driver.'

'He had diarrhoea,' *DS Preece offers.*

'We were briefed about not getting out of each others sight, and not using phone,' *DC Horn says sheepishly.*

'Oh fucking hell,' *DS Preece says at the prospect of a disciplinary charge before him now.*

'Let's go!' *the voice barks.*

DS Preece springs out of the car with DC Horn. They run off towards the target's house.

Three

'This is fucking outrageous, you cunts,' *Detective Sergeant Lenny Feast says angrily as he's brought into a small interview room by two detectives. He is large and sweating despite having kept himself in shape. He is only half dressed, shirtsleeves and trousers. One of the detectives with him is DC Roy Horn, the other is DS Preece.*

'I never heard anything so fucking outrageous,' *DS Feast continues.* 'What kind of a cunt d'you think I am? I've been a detective twenty years. Twenty years! Anyone would think I was a villain. You fucking yokels sure you nicked the right fella? I mean, you sure you hit the right address? I can't believe it, crashing the fucking door in. I mean, we pull them sort of strokes – it's fucking outrageous. Have you any idea how much that door cost? You little lot might live in cowsheds – that's a genuine imitation Georgian door fucking ruined!'

He looks at them and waits, as if expecting a response, but none is forthcoming from either detective.

'I'd better give my guvnor a bell, I mean, this is not on, is it,' *Feast says, moderating his tack.* 'I don't even know what the charge is. You wanna tell me why I'm nicked?'

There's no response.

'I mean, let's be sensible, friend,' *he says, making a reasonable appeal.* 'You could at least give me half a chance. Give me the SP, I mean, that's not unreasonable is it. Know what I mean, friend. You can be half decent towards a brother officer, can't you?'

He waits, with every expectation of his appeal getting a sympathetic response.

When it gets none at all, he says. 'You no-good, sheep-fucking cunts! There's not one of you worth a toss compared to Met officers – you could put fuck all away even if we put our hands up to it, you cunts. You might as well get on your bikes back to Wiltshire.'

Exasperated, frustrated by this lack of response, he turns away in disgust.

Detective Chief Inspector Brian Humpfress is short and stocky. He only just made the minimum height for the police.

'Pop that up to the super', Roy,' *he says to DC Horn, handing him a folder.*

DC Horn gets out.

'Sergeant,' *he says by way of greeting.* 'I'm Chief Inspector Humpfress . . .'

'Oh, pleased to meet you, sir,' *DS Feast says, expansively, extending his hand to shake his like he would an old friend's.* 'Detective Sergeant Lenny Feast . . . Very pleased to meet you, sir. I'm glad we've got a bit of rank at last, sir. I feel there's been a serious error made here, sir. A very serious error indeed.'

'Indeed there has, sergeant,' *DCI Humpfress says in the same reasonable tone.* 'And you're the one who's made it.'

'Me, sir?' *Feast says, incredulously.* 'But I've been a detective for twenty years. Without a stain on my record.'

'But one or two very narrow squeaks. Let's say you've been lucky.'

'Bloody hard-working, is what I've been, and this is all the thanks I get for it,' *Feast says, indignation creeping into his tone.*

'Something nearer the truth is, I'd say,' *DCI Humpfress tells him, rocking backwards and forwards on his cuban heels,* 'you're a very corrupt detective who's had a better than good run for his money.'

'That's ballocks,' *Feast tells him.*

'I'm pleased to hear it,' *Humpfress says,* 'It gives me no pleasure having to arrest policemen.'

During this DC Roy Horn comes into the office bringing with him a plastic bag of water-sodden banknotes. This he gives to Preece then goes out.

'How much is here, Del?' *DCI Humpfress*

asks, pulling some of the money from the bag, ignoring Feast now.

'Nearly three thousand pounds, boss,' *DS Preece says.* 'I don't know how much he managed to flush down the lav' before we collared him.'

The chief inspector glances at DS Feast. 'I thought London policemen were supposed to be smart. It looks like we got this bugger dead to rights, caught with his hand in the loo, so to speak. This isn't piss on these notes, is it?' *He says, quickly dropping them.*

'He wouldn't have had time for a piss as well, boss,' *DS Preece says.*

'No, I suppose not – by the way, Inspector Jobbins thinks it was your driver who tipped him off.' *DCI Humpfress tells him.*

DS Preece pulls a sheepish face. 'He was taken short boss.'

'We'll get to that later,' *he says.* 'Well, what do you have to say for yourself?'

He slides the money in the large glassine bag across the table where DS Feast is.

'There really has been a big mistake made here, sir.'

'I'd say,' *DCI Humpfress concedes.* 'An error of about three thousand pounds.'

'These cunts come crashing in in the middle of the night,' *DS Feast protests.* 'S'fucking outrageous, that sort of behaviour.'

'But what did they find?' *DCI Humpfress says.* 'You stuffing these banknotes down the loo.'

'Me?' *Feast says incredulously.* 'Don't talk fucking silly, guvnor. I *was* in the bathroom when they crashed in – had a bit of diarrhoea . . .'

'What's this – bumpaper?' *The DCI flicks casually at the money.* 'You blokes earn so much nowadays you can afford to wipe your arse on it.'

'No, you got it all wrong, guv,' *Feast says, changing his tack.*

'Are you denying this money was in your possession?' *DCI Humpfress wants to know.* 'Is that your position?'

DS Feast thinks about that, then nods. 'I'm saying I don't know anything about it.'

'How did it get into your lavatory?' *DCI Humpfress asks.*

'Well I could tell you it's the result of my rich diet. If you were reasonable Bill you'd accept that.' *DS Feast says.* 'But what most likely happened is these clods brought it with them.'

'You lying fucker . . .' *DS Preece says and punches him in the kidneys.*

DS Feast hangs breathlessly in the air for a second. As he does, DCI Humpfress slides a chair neatly in behind him and guides him down into it.

'You'd better sit down, friend,' *DCI Humpfress says.* 'Now why don't you stay calm and try to recall how that money came to be in the lavvy.'

Feast attempts to speak but can't get the words out for the winding effect of the punch.

'Take your time, sergeant. We've only been on this investigation a year. Who was first through the bathroom door, Del?' *he says turning to DS Preece.*

'I was boss, followed by Inspector Jobbins,' *DS Preece says.*

'S'my old woman's money,' *DS Feast at last manages breathlessly.*

'She won it on the horses, I daresay,' *DCI Humpfress says like he's heard this explanation a million times before.*

'I don't think so, guv – bingo.' *That sounds as breathless, but almost plausible. So much so that it stops DCI Humpfress for a moment.*

Humpfress nods. 'Why were you putting it down the lavatory?'

Feast thinks about that. 'I'm tryn'a stop her going to bingo. I said if she brought any more of her winnings home I'd burn them – well our new town house doesn't have a fireplace – know what I mean?'

'Supposing I were to tell you this is part of the proceeds of a robbery that took place at Coutts Bank, last November?' *DCI Humpfress says.*

'I'd say you were a fucking liar, pal,' *DS Feast insists.*

DCI Humpfress glances at his DS, as if about to turn him loose. DS Feast sees the look and tenses expectantly.

'That cunt pulls another fucking stroke. I'll knock him spark out,' *DS Feast says.*

'Don't be like that, sergeant,' *DCI Humpfress says, stepping back with a smile, like he doesn't want to be a part of this trouble.* 'We don't need that sort of behaviour.'

Sensing that he's getting on top of the situation, DS Feast tries to press his advantage. 'Just so we know where we stand.' *he says.* 'Right.'

'Just because we're on opposite sides of the fence, nothing says we can't behave decently, towards each other. Like brother officers,' *DCI Humpfress tells him.*

'I haven't been treated like that, dragged out of my bed . . .' *Feast jumps in.*

'Bathroom – you were in the bathroom,' *DS Preece reminds him.*

'Okay, bathroom – for all the fucking dif' it makes,' *Feast says.* 'But what I want to know is why I'm here; if I'm being nicked, what the charge is.'

'Yes, yes, yes. I'm sorry, sergeant. There's no reason to treat you as if you were a regular bad lad,' *DCI Humpfress reassures him.*

'I'd say so, guv,' *DS Feast says.*

'We should have behaved in a reasonably civilised fashion,' *Humpfress says,* '– called round at a decent hour, telephoning beforehand . . .'

'You'd have found me half-reasonable,' *Feast responds.*

DCI Humpfress nods. 'I'm sorry it's been like this, sergeant. Let me put you in the picture. You've been brought here to help us with our investigation into allegations of widespread police corruption. Your name was given us by no less than three criminals who have so far been charged with eighteen major robberies,' *DCI Humpfress says matter-of-factly.* 'As to the second part of your questions, yes, you can consider yourself pinched. The DPP has considered the papers, and believes there's an excellent chance of getting a conviction. So I'm now going to charge you Leonard John Feast that on or about the 20th November you did conspire with others unknown to rob Coutts Bank . . .'

'Leave off, for fuck sake. Leave off!' *DS*

Feast says with a sense of panic. 'You don't want to nick me. I don't know fuck all. I mean, what the fuck am I, a poxy DS? You want to nick someone, nick those hungry bastards what get the lion's share. They're the cunts that need nicking, not me . . . I mean, they're all at it, aren't they?'

The Operation Bad Apple detectives wait expectantly.

Having recovered his initial shock he starts to look for a way out. 'Well, the thing is, guv, if I'm expected to give you a few names, what good it's gonna do me. I mean, can I get some sort of help? And what sort of help am I likely to get?'

'I imagine some sort of help could be organised,' *DCI Humpfress tells him.* 'But it's all a question of what you give us, sergeant.'

'Oh I can put up the names of some detectives who are well at it,' *DS Feast assures him.*

'Like who for instance?' *the DCI asks hopefully.*

Feast gives a nervous laugh. 'Leave it out, guv. I mean, I'm prepared to sacrifice a few in order to save myself. But I've got to know I *can* save myself.'

'I'll ask my boss to talk to the assistant chief constable who's in charge of the investigation,' *DCI Humpfress says, after a moment's thought.* 'But understand this, I don't promise a thing.'

'No?' *Feast says, unsure about this, thinking, half-expecting that this man is joking.* 'But they will have to listen, though, pal won't they?'

The DCI considers him. There's an air of distaste for this. 'Take him down to the cells – get him some tea. I'll have a word with the chief superintendent,' *he says, leaving the room.*

'A bit of breakfast would be handy,' *DS Feast says, feeling himself retrieving the situation.*

DS Feast goes out with the two detectives.

Four

'How much do you feel this Sergeant Feast knows, Tony?' *Assistant Chief Constable*

Alan Leeper says as he approaches the vending machine parked in the corridor. He puts a coin in for coffee.

DCS Tony Bulmer begins cautiously, 'It certainly looks like he knows more than us. We've only been at it a year, he's been at it twenty years.'

'And he definitely wants to, does he?' *Leeper asks.*

'He wants to know what we're prepared to offer. How much he's holding back? Your guess is as good as mine,' *DCS Bulmer says.*

'They're hungry bastards up here, Tony,' *the assistant chief constable says. He's heavy, in his 50s, suffers high blood pressure.* 'It won't be cheap.'

'It could be if he's got the right answers. He wants to keep his pension.' *Bulmer puts his own coin in the machine.*

'He's offering us the *most* corrupt detectives in London?' *Assistant Chief Constable Leeper asks.*

'That's what he said,' *DCS Bulmer confirms.*

'That sounds very attractive, especially after all the foot-slogging done. Not that I want to see brother officers fall, not senior officers.'

'He might be bullshitting, Alan,' *DCS Bulmer says.*

'I can't guarantee Feast will keep his pension, but there's no reason to tell him that,' *Leeper says.* 'I'll put his offer up to the DPP. I imagine he'll play ball. Sir Trevor is as keen as we are to get someone with more rank. I'll see if I can reach him right away.'

They go off along the corridor with their coffee.

Five

DS Feast is brought into an interview room, looking more unkempt than when he was picked up, having been at the police station a full thirty-six hours. He is in need of a shave, a bath, some sleep. DS Del Preece is with him.

'I don't s'pose there's any chance of a cuppa tea, is there?' *Feast asks.* 'Them bastards down in the cells dropped me out this morning.'

'I should think we can arrange that,' *DS Preece says reasonably.*

DCI Brian Humpfress comes in with a thick folder.

'Are we on then?' *DS Feast asks, somewhat hopefully, having the appearance of being ground down.*

The DCI waits. But in vain. 'Forgotten something, sergeant, haven't you?'

'Sir,' *Feast adds after a moment.* 'Yes, sir.'

'Well if it was up to me, sergeant, I wouldn't give you the time of day,' *DCI Humpfress tells him.* 'I'd have you down in Brixton on remand, we've got so much evidence. But that's what makes my boss so interested.'

DCS Tony Bulmer strides in. He's tall, willowy, with a slight stoop; in his early fifties. He slaps his hands together. 'Right,' *he says,* 'you want to do a little horse-trading?'

'It would be useful, sir', *Feast says.* 'I have put up a lot of information.'

'All this lot looks like,' *Bulmer says, taking a folder from DCI Humpfress and opening it,* 'is a list of senior detectives, nothing more.'

'Well that's what it is, sir,' *Feast says.* 'But I mean, they're all at it.'

'That's what most villains are telling us,' *DCS Bulmer points out.* 'But without much evidence to support such statements.'

'But I gave you details of what they've been having,' *Feast explains.*

'So have villains. As the DPP pointed out, there's nothing here that gives anything like the chance of conviction he wants,' *DCS Bulmer explains.*

'Fuck I!' *DS Feast says.* 'What does he want, signed confessions? We've stuck villains up on a lot less, and got a result. A bit of verbal always helps. That's the way you do it.'

'But here we'd be dealing with senior officers, who have hitherto unblemished records. Consider this man for instance, Chief Inspector Sneed. He has,' *he counts* 'twelve commendations. One from the queen no less.'

'Cor, fucking hell. Terry Sneed!' *Feast insists.* 'He's gotta be the bentest Old Bill around.'

DCS Bulmer considers him. 'Are you telling

us the queen was wrong in giving this commendation? Is that what you're telling us? He'd stand by his record and get the case thrown out of court.' *He shakes his head.* 'It's just not on, old son.'

'Fuck I! I thought I was gonna have a right result,' *Feast says.*

'Of course if he was to reconsider going into the witness-box himself?' *DCI Humpfress offers.*

'There's no way I'm gonna stay in the job and keep my pension, I do that.' *DS Feast says.* 'I mean, not if I get up and say I know this officer and that officer were involved, 'cos I had some too.'

'Then what do you suggest, sergeant?' *DCS Bulmer says.*

'To be perfectly honest, sir,' *Feast says,* 'I'm fucked if I know.'

'What we have here is an impasse,' *DCS Bulmer says.* 'On the one hand there's you, a smelly little fish in a big stinking pool; you're truly hooked and wriggling to get free. On the other hand there's us; we're well and truly fed up with little tiddlers, specially when we know the big fish are swimming free. Your problem is there's no way you can get them onto our hook and set yourself free. Our problem is we can't achieve that either, not without you getting swallowed.' *The DCS pauses.* 'Would you agree that sums up the situation?'

Feast agrees with a shrug. 'Just about.'

He gathers up the folder on Feast and passes it to DCI Humpfress, whom he now addresses. 'I think we're going to have to make do with one more small fish, Brian.'

'It looks that way, boss,' *the DCI says.*

'Leave off, guv,' *DS Feast says.* 'I mean, I didn't want to be involved. They put a gun to your head, you're either on the firm or out of work.'

'Well? Are you prepared to go into the witness-box?' *DCS Bulmer says.*

DS Feast shakes his head. 'I like being a policeman too much.'

'You're not going to be a policeman for much longer anyway.' *Bulmer tells him.*

'I've got half a chance,' *Feast says optimistically.*

He gathers up his papers, ignoring Feast

now. 'Did you get any joy with that witness from Brixton, Brian?' *he asks DCI Humpfress as they go out.*

'Yes, he gave us a couple of names.'

Their departure leaves DS Feast puzzled.

'What's this, a fucking get up?' *he says.* 'I mean, where's he going?'

'The chief superintendent's a busy man,' *DS Preece tells him.*

'I wasn't wasting his time,' *Feast says, self-justifyingly.* 'I mean, you could see that, couldn't you.I'm just tryn'a get some deal for myself that's all. I mean I'm entitled to try, aren't I?'

'That's only natural,' *DS Preece says.* 'We all do it.'

''Course we do,' *Feast says, beginning to live again through this man's favourable opinion of him.*

'Do you want the super' to help after all, do you?' *DS Preece offers.*

'Get him back here,' *Feast says.*

'He's a busy man, Lenny,' *DS Preece says.*

'I'll do the business for him,' *Feast says.*

DS Del Preece nods approvingly, then goes out.

Left to his own devices, DS Feast is not a happy man. He's full of twitches and unpleasant mannerisms.

There's almost joy on his face when DS Preece returns with DCS Bulmer.

'What do you want?' *DCS Bulmer says without prelusive niceties.*

'I'll do the business,' *Feast insists.*

'You'll go into the witness-box?' *Bulmer says.*

'Anything but that, guv,' *Feast says. When he sees his interrogators' doubting looks,* 'I mean anything, you name it.'

'The only alternative would be for you to get fresh evidence on these policemen,' *DCS Bulmer asks.*

'I'll do that all right. How's it done?' *Feast wants to know.*

'With a wire. You arrange to meet with these policemen, get them to talk about their criminal enterprises, all of which you'll record with a concealed microphone,'

Bulmer explains.

'Just like that?' *DS Feast says, dismayed at their naivety.* 'I mean that won't be difficult, they've only just got off the boat.'

'That's your problem, Lenny,' *Bulmer says.* 'If you can't do it then there's no help for you.'

'Oh I'll give it a go, I've got to,' *Feast says.*

DCS Bulmer nods. 'I'll get the assistant chief constable to have a word with the DPP, get them to send the papers back marked pending.'

'It might take a little while, sir,' *DS Feast says.* 'To collect that sort of information.'

'Understand this, any agreement the DPP enters into is entirely dependent upon results,' *the DCS warns him.*

'I understand, sir,' *DS Feast says, accepting the deal.*

'Good,' *Bulmer says.*

Darkness.

Six

At the bar of a fairly quiet pub a villain in his forties, Brian Cayman, stands drinking. He's alert, his eyes flicking around the room. He's thin and wears a velvet collared overcoat. Detective Chief Inspector Terry Sneed comes out of the gents and joins Cayman at the bar, where his glass of scotch is waiting.

'That's handy, Brian,' *Detective Chief Inspector Sneed says, brushing his thumbs down his inside pocket, which now contains Cayman's money.* 'Helps towards a new engine for the boat.'

Cayman looks at him, not enjoying the detective's smiling, relaxed manner when he is in trouble himself. 'The thing is, what sort of help does that bit of money get me?'

'Fuck all I'd say,' *Sneed tells him.* 'This is what got me here listening to your troubles in these dangerous times, Brian.' *He swallows some scotch.* 'What's the SP?'

'I had word I'm about to be nicked,' *Cayman says.*

'I'd say you were about due, you been at it long enough,' *Sneed observes.* 'When and where is this supposed to happen?'

'I don't know when,' *Cayman tells him.* 'The DS on the case said they had a grass who was lollying anyone and everyone he could think of. S'over the water – Southwark.'

'What's involved, Brian?' *Sneed asks.*

'I was on the firm what tucked up that bonded warehouse last month. Comes to about sixty grand,' *Cayman says.*

'I don't suppose that'd be enough to go into those hungry bastards over there,' *Sneed comments, apparently disinterested.*

'There's more aggravation than enough trying to do the business with Operation Bad Apple around,' *Cayman complains.*

'It's fucking everything,' *Sneed tells him.* 'So what the fuck d'you expect me to do, make them go away?'

'I thought if anyone can do anything, Terry,' *Cayman says.*

'I don't think so, Brian. Those cunts are worrying everyone,' *Sneed tells him.* 'I mean, I know detectives who have never been straight turning away earners nowadays.'

'S'just my fucking form,' *Cayman says.* 'There'd be plenty of dough on offer too.'

'Business can still be done, Brian, don't get me wrong,' *Sneed says, changing his tack.* 'It just costs more, that's all. Won't your man do anything?'

'He needs the money, but he's shit scared,' *Cayman says.* 'It was as much as he'd do to give me a bell.'

'You could always leg it, Brian,' *Sneed tells him.*

'Fuck that. S'right mug's game.'

'I'd say so. D'you stick anyone up for it – a body?' *Sneed asks casually, interrogating this man from habit.*

'Oh yeah, 'course. We give the filth an old mug,' *he says like that is now obligatory to any robbery.*

'Is he putting your name up?' *Sneed asks.*

'I wouldn't think so, Terry. Bad Apple nicked some other no-good cunt and promised him the earth for a few names. I think he's sticking up more than enough bent Old Bill an' all.'

'It sounds well involved. What are you looking for, Brian?' *Sneed asks*. 'Bit of help in court?'

'Bollocks!' *Cayman says*. 'I could get that by lollying a few myself. To be honest, Terry, I'd be looking to get dropped right out.'

'You might be asking a bit too much there,' *Sneed says*.

'Well the thing is, Terry, the only other get out for me would be to talk to them other cunts, stick a few Old Bill up myself. I mean, I know more than enough who are at it,' *Cayman says, trying to blackmail Sneed*.

Sneed considers him for a moment. 'Why don't you do that, uncle,' *Sneed challenges*. 'It sounds like the smart move to me. I mean, they'll listen to you.'

He waits, watching Brian Cayman, who doesn't enjoy this challenge.

'You might just have to wipe your mouth, son. Maybe do a bit of bird,' *Sneed says*.

'S'right fucking sick'ner.' *Cayman says*.

Sneed nods. 'You got plenty of dough tucked away, Brian?' *he asks reasonably*.

'A bit. I mean, enough, I got enough to weigh on for some help.'

'There's a couple CID I could go into for you. But they won't come cheap, Brian. I'd want a nice earner myself,' *Sneed says*.

'That won't be a problem,' *Cayman tells him*.

'As long as you don't try and weigh on with that bent scotch,' *Sneed advises*.

'That's well gone, to a supermarket chain – they stick it in their own bottles. We are talking about me being dropped right out?' *Cayman clarifies*. 'Not just sticking up some favourable verbal in court.'

'Fuck all value if you're still in the frame, is it,' *Sneed says*. 'We're talking about three grand.'

'Fuck I! That's nearly all my whack.' *Cayman is dismayed at the price.*

'S'terrible, isn't it,' *Sneed commiserates*. 'But what can you do?'

'But three grand.' *He wants to negotiate with this detective but is scared to as this is the only offer of help he's had. With a reluctant nod, Brian Cayman accepts the deal.*

'I'll have a word with a detective out of Southwark – see what can be done,' *Sneed says. He swallows the rest of his scotch and goes out.*

Cayman stays on and thinks about his deal. He shakes his head, then finishes his drink and leaves.

Seven

'It's like I told you on the phone, Terry,' *DS Lenny Feast says, coming into a small office carrying a cup of tea, followed by DCI Sneed, who also has tea.* 'I don't think anything can be done for Brian Cayman, not with them other cunts from Wiltshire making themselves busy. I mean, I even got a spin the other week.'

'I heard,' *Sneed says*.

Feast seizes upon this in a paranoid way. 'What did you hear?' *he wants to know*.

'I heard you got turned over.'

Feast says, 'What else did you hear? There's no stories going around about me, are there? No one's saying I'm a grass?'

'Would I fucking well be here talking like this?' *Sneed says*. 'How d'you go anyway?'

'The cunts were well out of order. They had to wipe their mouths. But it makes your bottle go, Terry, makes you think whether it's worth the few quid you earn the other way – what sort of dough would your man be talking about?'

'It's got to come to a grand, 'he can be dropped right out,' *Sneed says*.

'Bit more than that I'd've said, Terry,' *DS Feast tells him*. 'It'll be well involved – my guvnor won't put himself on offer for that sort of dough. It's gotta come to two, I'd've said.'

'Two grand would be all right,' *Sneed confirms*.

'We are talking about the scotch out of the Tooley Street warehouse?' *Feast says for the mike*.

Sneed nods. 'He wants dropping right out.'

'I think the business can be done all right,' *DS Feast says*. 'Has he been into any of the detectives on the case?'

'There's a DS called Wadswater,' *Sneed says.*

'Morry Wadswater? He's well bent. Wouldn't he do nothing?' *Feast asks him.*

'Said he couldn't, not with those other cunts looking to nick every Old Bill that drew breath,' *Sneed says.*

'I'll have a word – how is DS Wadswater involved?' *Feast asks.*

'He nicked the body Cayman's little firm stuck up,' *Steed explains.*

'Was everyone else involved, Terry?' *Feast asks.*

'Wadswater's governor had a taste, so Brian Cayman reckons,' *Sneed says.*

'How much did Inspector Pinnock have?' *Feast asks.*

Sneed looks at him. 'You can't rely on what villains tell you,' *he says.* 'What's that got to do with anything?'

'I don't know,' *DS Feast says, recovering his surprise.* 'If you're saying he was bunged a few quid, I'd need to know how much for when I go into him again.'

'If he fancies a drink he'll go again on it, won't he,' *Sneed says.* 'The amount he had before won't make the dif'.'

'Well, I don't know, it might,' *Feast is uncomfortable with this line of questioning.*

'What's the matter with you, Lenny? You look like you're shitting yourself,' *Sneed observes. His statements aren't in fact pregnant with suspicion, but that's Feast's interpretation.*

'It's them other cunts, Terry. They're enough to make your arse go,' *Feast says.*

'They've been making themselves double busy at the Yard,' *Sneed says.* 'They've nicked fuck all though.'

'There are a few in the frame, Terry,' *Feast says.*

'They've scratched no deeper than that,' *Sneed says, scratching the table top.* 'They couldn't capture goldfish out of a garden pond.'

'Still, I think we should have our next meet' away from here,' *Feast suggests.* 'All right.'

'I'll make the arrangements for the bit of dough.' *Sneed wrinkles his nose in disgust at* the tea. 'This fucking tea's putrid. What's that old tart in the canteen do, piss in it?' *He sets the cup down.* 'Where'll I find DCI Middleton?'

'He's upstairs. I'll show you – what he's having, Terry?' *Feast asks.*

'His old lady, I s'pose,' *Sneed says cautiously.* 'Give me a bell when your ready to do the biz.'

They go out.

Eight

DCS Tony Bulmer and DCI Humpfress and Assistant Chief Constable Alan Leeper come into the latter's temporary office. DCI Humpfress has a tape on a cassette recorder which he rewinds, looking for a particular section.

'How reliable is this information we're getting from Chief Inspector Sneed?' *the assistant chief constable asks, hanging up his coat.*

'Most of it ties in with what we're picking up elsewhere,' *DCS Bulmer says.*

'He has every appearance of being a very corrupt policeman,' *Leeper says.* 'What sort of man is DCI Sneed?'

Fetching up on the cassette player at this point Sneed is saying 'Those cunts from Wiltshire'll just have to go back to fucking sheep . . .' *much to everyone's embarrassment.*

DCI Humpfress says, 'He's very efficient.' *Having found the spot he wants on the tape, he pauses it.* 'A bit remote. Won't let anyone get close to him. Academically he's always done well. He's expected to get his promotion to superintendent at his next board.'

'That seems like a tragic waste. Are we ready to pick him up?' *Assistant Chief Constable Leeper says.* 'I wouldn't like this one alerted like so many of the others.'

Humpfress says, 'Feast has arranged another meeting. He's looking to Sneed for help for a third party this time.'

'Our detectives *will* be in whistling distance, Alan,' *DCS Bulmer assures him.*

'I'd prefer them to be in the bar with Feast,'

Leeper says.

'I don't think we dare risk that, Alan,' *DCS Bulmer says.* 'Sneed's a cagey bugger. He'd spot them right away.'

'Let's hear the relevant bit,' *the assistant chief constable says.*

DCI Humpfress presses the start button.

'. . . Cayman will be dropped out. Don't think they'll be any problem with those other cunts. Not now Harry Stern is in the frame,' *Sneed's voice says out of the cassette player.*

'Did Superintendent Stern know that the blag at Harrod's was going off?' *Feast's voice asks.*

There's a pause.

'What do you think, Lenny?' *Sneed's voice.*

'The mind boggles at just who might be on the firm . . .' *Feast's voice.*

'It does indeed,' *Leeper puts in.*

'Is that the time?' *Sneed's voice says.* 'We've got a joint raid with the RCS. I'm doing the briefing.'

'You think you can help out on that other business with Rogers, if the price is right . . ?' *Feast's voice is asking as the tape runs out.*

'Is that it?' *the assistant chief constable says.*

'I'm afraid the tape ran out, Alan,' *DCS Bulmer says.*

'Why doesn't he take longer tapes to these meetings?' *the assistant chief constable asks.* 'This is ridiculous.'

'A question of concealment, sir,' *DCI Humpfress says.* 'Longer tapes means bigger machines.'

Leeper says, 'Can't this Feast character switch it on when Sneed says something incriminating?'

'We mustn't underestimate Mr Sneed,' *the DCS says.* 'This business with Rogers is something we'll know about as soon as Sneed moves on it,' *DCS Bulmer explains.* 'We've set it up.'

'I can't say I like that,' *the assistant chief constable says.* 'But I suppose it must be done.'

'The end justifies the means, I dare say, Alan,' *DCS Bulmer says, releasing the tape with a snap.*

'Just as long as it doesn't backfire,' *the assistant chief constable says.* 'The consequences are frightening.'

'Sergeant Feast reckons,' *DCS Bulmer says,* 'if we manage to crack Sneed there'll hardly be a detective in London left untouched.'

'That's what I mean, Tony. Chief Inspector Sneed might prove too hot for everyone. I'd best let the DPP hear this one,' *he says, taking the tape.*

They go out of the office.

Nine

'It's quiet enough here, Terry,' *DS Feast says as he comes and sits at a corner table in a bar room with Sneed. Both have drinks in their hands.* 'I began to get worried,' 'didn't hear from you. I mean, Gordon Rogers could go up the steps anytime. We'd've fucking job doing the business once he's sent down. Unless you can go into the judge.'

'Inflation affects them like everyone else,' *Sneed replies.*

'Well I don't know any Old Bill ever going into a judge – magistrates okay,' *Feast says. DS Feast waits but Sneed isn't forthcoming.* 'D'you ever come across judges you could bung a few quid to, Terry?'

Sneed looks at him. 'D'you get the dough for chummy's bit of help?' *he asks.*

'Fifteen hundred sovs.' *Feast says, patting his coat pocket where there's a bulge behind his folded newspaper.* 'D'you wanna cop it in the karsey, Terry?'

Sneed shakes his head. 'We were talking about two and a half grand, not one and a half,' *he says coldly.*

'Rogers wants to see the sort of help you get him in court before he comes up with the other grand,' *DS Feast tells him.*

'What d'you take me for, a cunt?' *DCI Sneed says.* 'When a fucking villain makes a deal with me for some help, that's the fucking deal, or there's no help.'

'He's as good as gold, Terry,' *Feast insists.*

'You're taking me for a right fucking wolly, uncle,' *Sneed says, finishing his drink, making to leave.*

'No, I'm not. I'm not, Terry, I wouldn't do that.' *Lenny Feast is getting a bit desperate.*

'Well I promise you one thing, son, your fucking pal Rogers is going to top up being well and truly verballed.' *Sneed starts to rise.*

'Don't be like that, Tel. Be sensible, cop the one and half – I'll get the other bit for you tonight.'

'Ballocks,' *Sneed says.* 'I won't be fucked around.'

'Don't be snaky, Tel. Look, take that for your trouble, Terry,' *Feast says, trying to stuff the package of money into Sneed's pocket.* 'Have another drink . . .'

'You cunt! What's your fucking game – is this a set-up . . . ?' *Sneed says, pushing him off as Feast tries to restrain him. As he does so he feels something in Feast's sleeve that he instantly recognises.* 'You dirty no-good cunt,' *he says, ripping at his coat.* 'You got a fucking wire on! You cunt. . .' *He rips furiously, exposing the tape machine that is strapped to Feast.* 'What did you do that for? What d'you do it for?' *A desperate fury rising in Sneed.*

'Don't be snaky, Terry, they got a gun to me head . . .' *Feast explains.* 'I had to. I had to!'

'You cunt! How much you got?' *Sneed explodes, still trying to bodily rip the recorder from Feast.*

The two detectives are fighting now, Feast trying to protect both himself and his interest as they wrestle on the floor.

'Switch it off! Switch it off!' *Sneed screams.*

'They nicked me, Terry, they have a gun to m' head . . .' *It's a desperate appeal for understanding by Feast.*

'You're nicked, you cunt. You're nicked!' *Sneed tries.* 'I'm arresting you for tryin' a pervert the course of justice . . .'

The bar manager has arrived by this time. 'Stop this,' *he says,* 'or I'll call the police.'

'I am the police,' *DS Feast says.* 'I'm arresting this man, – help me. Please help me, I'm arresting him.'

'You're nicked, you're fucking nicked,' *Sneed says, as if saying the words was important.*

At this point DCI Humpfress, DS Preece

and DC Horn burst in to render some assistance. Humpfress keeps well back and speaks into his personal radio while the others wade in to arrest Sneed.*

'Leave off you cunts,' *Sneed cries.* 'I just nicked him.'

Sneed resists arrest.

'Where're the cuffs?' *DS Preece asks. They have a fight on their hands with Sneed now, he's not going to come peaceably.*

'I thought you had them, skip,' *DC Horn says.*

'No you were supposed to bring them, you berk,' *Preece says.*

'No you were supposed to bring them, you berk,' *Preece says.*

They are sitting on Sneed by this time, slamming their knees into him to stop his resistance.

'Give me a chance, for fuck sake. We're all policemen after all,' *Sneed says.*

'Hold him can't you, hold him . . .' *DS Preece says.*

'Everything is under control here,' *DCI Humpfress says into his radio.* 'I've made the arrest.'

'You got any handcuffs?' *DS Preece says to DS Feast.*

Sheepishly Feast passes over a pair of handcuffs. Preece clamps them onto Sneed's wrists, then they get up off him, bringing Sneed up.

Sneed considers the detectives, 'Nice bastards, you lot. There's no need for these *(cuffs)*, I'm not an animal.' *Then he turns to DS Feast.* 'You're nicked, uncle,' *he says.* 'I guarantee you'll stay nicked, whatever these cunts have promised you.'

Feast doesn't respond.

'Nice to see you've kept your sense of humour,' *DCI Humpfress says to Sneed, flexing his shoulders.*

Sneed considers him. 'We'll see,' *he says, putting on a confident front.*

'Take him to the car,' *Humpfress tells his detective. He waits while Sneed is taken out. Then he turns to the manager, who stands gaping, and gives him a reassuring smile.*

'Sorry about the disturbance, sir, the

excitement is all over now,' *he says.*

'Oh well, ah no harm done, sir,' *the manager says. He stands a chair up then goes.*

'That was close,' *DCI Humpfress observes to Feast.*

'He will stay nicked? Will he?' *Feast asks.*

'I wouldn't lose sleep over that,' *the DCI reassures him.*

'Well, I mean, I'm finished in the job otherwise. I mean, word goes round that I'm not only a grass, but I fitted him,' *Feast says.*

Humpfress laughs. 'You'll probably end up with a commissioner's commendation – after all that bent bastard got eleven of them.' *He picks up the tape recorder.* 'Did you get him to take the money to pay Superintendent Stern?'

'No,' *DS Feast says, indicating the package on the table.* 'It's there. I mean I should've had the full amount, he'd have taken it then.'

'But you'd have had no reason for seeing him again,' *Humpfress says, picking up the money.* 'Still, it's not the end of the world. We'll give it to him at the station. That'll do just as well.'

He goes out of the bar room, followed by Feast.

Ten

'I think the evidence you've managed to get from this detective is first rate,' *AC Peter Vyvyan says coming into his office and putting on the light. Assistant Chief Constable Leeper is with him.* 'So hot in fact I didn't even like having it in my office.' *He unlocks the drawer of his desk and removes the tape. Having been got en route to a dinner function he is dressed in black velvet collared overcoat and white silk scarf.*

'This is the break we've been waiting for all these months,' *Assistant Chief Constable Leeper says.* 'I don't mind telling you I began to have my doubts about ever cracking this investigation.'

'I don't mind telling you,' *Peter Vyvyan says,* 'we all had our doubts. This calls for a small celebratory drink.' *He looks at his watch.* 'Yes, there's time. I'm giving a

speech to the Bar Association on the most effective means of policing the Metropolis. I only wish I knew what they were!' *He takes a bottle of scotch and two glasses from a metal cupboard.*

'I don't normally,' *Assistant Chief Constable Leeper says.* 'The doctor told me to stay off drink on account of my high blood pressure.'

'Just a small one,' *AC Vyvyan says, pouring the drinks.* 'You deserve a well earned holiday.'

'Yes, I have one planned.' *He takes the drink.*

'Here's to a swift conclusion to Operation Bad Apple,' *Peter Vyvyan says.* 'Who was the detective on the tape by the way – his name wasn't mentioned?'

'Chief Inspector Sneed,' *the assistant chief constable says.*

AC Peter Vyvyan almost chokes on his scotch. It takes him a moment to recover himself. 'Terry Sneed . . . ?' *he coughs some more.* 'That went down the wrong way,' *he manages to say.*

'He's at the Yard here, possibly you know him,' *Assistant Chief Constable Leeper says innocently.*

Peter Vyvyan is vigorously shaking his head. 'He's newly arrived, is he?'

'No that's what so surprising,' *Assistant Chief Constable Leeper says.* 'He's been here two years.'

'Oh it's probably his first time,' *AC Vyvyan ventures.*

'This one's been bent for a very long time, Assistant Commissioner,' *Leeper says.* 'And before we're through we'll know who else is involved.'

'There might be difficulties with this sort of evidence,' *AC Vyvyan says, his attitude taking a sharp turn as he reaches the tapes back.* 'The problem is that on its own it won't mean very much.'

'We have every intention of getting this evidence corroborated,' *Assistant Chief Constable Leeper tells him.* 'We believe we've tapped a major source of corruption.'

'Possibly, but whether it'll hold up in court,' *– he shakes his head.* 'These certainly contain some interesting information. I can understand your excitement. I felt the same way when I listened to the tapes, I wanted to act immediately. But you probably know better than me, Mr Leeper, fools rush in.' *He considers the tapes.* 'While I don't believe that this Chief Inspector . . . what's his name . . . ?'

'Sneed,' *Assistant Chief Constable Leeper offers.*

'While I don't believe that he knew he was being recorded by Feast, I do think he is naturally cautious. There's little that's conclusive on these; sufficient for the DPP to satisfactorily prosecute.'

'What are you suggesting?' *Assistant Chief Constable Leeper asks, frustrated by this turn about.* 'That we let him go?'

'Unless you're very careful, you might have to,' *AC Vyvyan says.* 'There's no doubt that the man is a thorough rascal. But if you move too swiftly, you may inadvertently tip your hand.'

'It's a bit too late for that. He's in police cells,' *Assistant Chief Constable Leeper points out.*

'Oh, I see,' *Vyvyan says a little alarmed. Then recovering himself,* 'Excellent. That's where he should remain. But I suggest that if you want to bring a successful conclusion to this protracted investigation, you find something substantial to corroborate this evidence. Has the DPP heard these?' *he asks, picking up the tapes again.*

'Not yet. I was hoping to see him or his deputy tomorrow,' *Assistant Chief Constable Leeper says.*

'I'm seeing Sir Trevor this evening. I'll find a quiet moment and have a word,' *AC Vyvyan says, accepting no argument.* 'Think nothing of it, that'll be my small contribution. The DPP can advise you first thing in the morning.' *He slips the tapes into his pocket.* 'Now I must get along – the traffic in the West End is ridiculous. The uniform forces are doing nothing to deal with it,' *he says as they go out.*

Eleven

DCI Humpfress comes into the interview room and sits at the small table. He opens some of the very thick folders of cases he has brought with him. He skim reads as DCI Terry Sneed is brought in scuffing his feet to keep on his laceless shoes, and holding onto his beltless trousers. DS Preece is with him.

'Have a seat,' *Humpfress says, glancing up, then jumping up and flexing his shoulders, not enjoying Sneed standing over him.* 'Some of your past cases make very interesting reading. From these one might almost believe you paid criminals to plead guilty.'

'You treat suspects fairly and decently, they'll put their hand up for you,' *Sneed says ironically.*

'I think you'll find we treat you fair,' *DCI Humpfress tells him.* 'I see no point sending people to prison without good cause.'

'It's amazing,' *Sneed exclaims, his irony increasing.* 'S'absolutely fucking amazing. S'like sitting here listening to myself. Makes me feel very reassured, to know I'm dealing with straight policemen.'

'Well in that case perhaps you'd like to make a statement,' *DCI Humpfress suggests.* 'We could get this wrapped up in no time at all.'

'I told you last night, I'd be more than happy to make a statement if I had something to state,' *Sneed says.*

'I daresay we'll find something in this little lot,' *Humpfress says, flicking the files.*

'Might take a long, long time, uncle,' *Sneed warns him.*

'Oh we've all the time we need,' *Humpfress says, a note of bitterness creeping in.* 'It's only our children that are growing old without us and our marriages going to pot.'

'S'all part of the job,' *Sneed replies.* 'Word is the brass is looking to close up this whole fucking investigation.'

'That sounds like wishful thinking,' *DCI Humpfress says.* 'I only wish it were true.'

'S'not exactly a lot of progress, is there. A couple low ranking detectives isn't a lot to show for fourteen months' work,' *Sneed comments.*

'I daresay you know more about that than me, chief Inspector,' *he says sarcastically.* 'But you're not exactly a low ranking policeman. In fact you're a very senior officer. You could save all concerned a lot of time and trouble?'

'Time's not a problem, uncle,' *Sneed says.* 'I've got about ten years before I'm entitled to retire.'

'Come on, old son, make a clean breast of things,' *Humpfress encourages.* 'You know it'll make you feel better.'

'Like having a good shit?' *Sneed says.*

'I always feel better afterwards,' *DCI Humpfress tells him.* 'I cheated on my wife once, I had to finally tell her, I couldn't live with it.'

'Yeah? What did she say?' *Sneed asks.*

Humpfress looks at him a moment. 'Never you mind – but it made her feel better too.'

'Why the fuck don't you go back to Ambridge and plant your shallots?' *Sneed says.* 'We had no problem sorting out our wrong-doers before you lot got here.'

'There's no better time to get it off your chest, chief inspector. Everyone from my boss to the DPP is looking to sort this one out with the minimum of fuss,' *Humpfress says. DCS Bulmer enters during this and listens.*

'Are you putting some sort of deal on offer?' *Sneed asks, as if interested.*

'I don't have the authority to make a deal with you. But I'm sure your information will get every consideration,' *Humpfress says, drawn into this.*

Sneed says. 'Let's just suppose for a minute that I am agreeable. How about if I were to go into your assistant chief constable wired up like that agent provocateur you put onto me, and got him to put his hands up to unlawful intercourse with sheep? You think we might do a bit of trading?' *Sneed wants to know.*

'Unlawful intercourse with sheep! Are you fucking mad?' *DCI Humpfress says, springing up from his chair.*

'Is that what you're saying happened?' *DCS Bulmer asks. He has with him a fat folder file.*

'Isn't that why country coppers are issued with Wellington boots?' *Sneed says, purposely miscontruing the question.*

'I doubt if the crimes of country coppers ever amounted to anything more serious,' *DCS Bulmer says, as though he believes minor crimes of public figures are acceptable.* 'So how about it, chief inspector?'

'This is all ballocks. You must have sent your grass into the wrong man,' *Sneed says.*

'I suppose that is an understandable reaction,' *DCS Bulmer says.*

'I'd hate to think what the right man might have been up to,' *DCI Humpfress says, with a smile.* 'If this is what we get from a random test, we've obviously been going about things the wrong way.'

'I've heard it said, Brian, that looking for corruption in the Met's like drilling for water in Ireland; no matter where you punch a hole it simply spurts out,' *DCS Bulmer says.* 'I think we've tapped a very deep spring.'

'What you've done, uncle, is made a very serious error,' *Sneed tries putting on a confident front, despite feeling sick at heart.*

'What we have on those tapes is enough to put you away for twenty years,' *Bulmer says.*

'You're talking to me like I'm a fucking wolly,' *Sneed protests, suddenly wearying of this line.* 'I'm thirty-five years old; I've been in the job as long as you. I tell you, uncle, if you had enough evidence to charge me, you'd have put it to me by now. I mean I've been where you are dozens of times myself, and with more worthwhile suspects.'

'I admire your confidence' *DCS Bulmer says.* 'I'd sooner deal with that than have them whimpering like some. Your friend Feast, he's a whimp. Cried like a baby to save himself. Is that right, Brian?'

'We had to fetch a mop in here,' *DCI Humpfress says.*

'It affects a lot like that,' *Sneed puts in, playing their game.* 'I've known some of the hardest villains who'd've let me fuck them up the arse for a bit of help.'

'Be interesting to see which way you go,' *DCS Bulmer says.*

'It's odds on that you've been into the DPP with those tapes,' *Sneed expounds.* 'He's listened to them, deliberated and finally come down on the side of caution. Tell me I'm wrong.'

The Bad Apple detectives don't respond.

'Fuck knows how many conversations that snaky cunt Feast recorded, but what I do know is that there's nothing on those tapes worth a toss.'

'The facts speak for themselves, chief inspector,' *Bulmer tells him simply, refusing to be rattled.*

'If it's facts you want, uncle', *Sneed counters,* 'I'm happy to let my record speak for me.'

'It is certainly impressive,' *Bulmer allows, opening one of the folders which contains Sneed's record.* 'That's what makes this all the more tragic, Terry. Is it all right if I call you Terry? I'm Tony, he's Brian,' *indicating DCI Humpfress. He turns to the third Operation Bad Apple detective whose name he can't remember.*

'It's Del, sir,' *DS Preece prompts.*

'Del, of course,' *Bulmer says.* 'How's the wife, Del? Had her baby yet?'

'The daughter's fifteen now, boss,' *DS Preece tells him.*

'Fifteen, of course she is.' *Feeling he's retrieved the situation, Bulmer moves on.* 'I'm surprised you'd risk such a fine career for a few measly pounds, Terry.'

'What am I s'pose to say to that, no it wasn't a few quid, we're talking about bundles?' *Sneed offers.*

Bulmer says. 'We could note that down for the verbals. That'll sound very promising in court. When I said to the defendant, I'm surprised you risked such a fine career for a few measly pounds, he replied, "No, it wasn't a few quid, we're talking about bundles of money".'

'Don't talk like a cunt, Tony,' *Sneed tells him.* 'The only surprise in all this is sending that bent cunt in to fit me. That's diabolical what you've done with Feast. A bit fucking swift.'

'You're the fit-up specialist,' *Bulmer says.* 'So rumour has it. If you've one that's a bit dodgy, let Terry Sneed look it over.'

'You know as well as I do, Tony, some villains need a little help up the river. Has to be done,' *Sneed says.*

'Oh I agree,' *DCS Bulmer says.* 'If the arresting officer were left to his own devices, there'd be a lot more bad lads behind bars.'

'I've had more than a few I've let go up on the evidence as it stood,' *Sneed said,* 'only to

have them get a result.'

'We all learn by our mistakes,' *Bulmer says.*

'Some do,' *Sneed says.*

'All right, let's stop playing silly buggers, shall we,' *Bulmer says, his patience deserting him. He flicks open a file.* 'Brian Cayman, the name's familiar?'

'Who?' *Sneed says.*

'Brian Cayman. He's an armed robber out of Bickley,' *Bulmer says.*

'Oh Brian Cayman,' *Sneed responds as if admitting knowing him. Then:* 'Never heard of him' – *dashing any expectation he may have offered.*

'You contacted DS Feast on Cayman's behalf to get him dropped from an investigation. He had robbed a bonded warehouse of £80,000 worth of whisky,' *Bulmer informs him.*

'Well, I'd be entitled to a drink out of that,' *Sneed jokes.*

This falls stone flat on the three detectives.

'Peter Rogers,' *DCS Bulmer says.*

'I know Peter,' *Sneed says.* 'He's a blagger. He's waiting to go up the steps for robbing a bank in Wimbledon.'

'You were in charge of that investigation,' *DCS Bulmer says.*

'We had a very nice result,' *Sneed puts in.*

'The fact is you were given Rogers by the other members of the gang, along with seven thousand pounds, which you planted on him,' *Bulmer says.*

'You're absolutely fucking amazing,' *Sneed says, appearing amazed.* 'You got all this evidence. Why don't you nick me?'

'I hold no particular brief for Rogers. Prison is where he belongs and I don't mind how he gets there. It's his misfortune that his confederates are such slippery turds. To be honest, Terry, my only interest is in using him as a stick to beat you with.'

'That makes sense, Tony,' *Sneed allows.*

'He's only too willing to be used in that way now it's been explained to him how he was fitted up,' *DCS Bulmer tells him.*

'That's ballocks,' *Sneed argues.* 'He was well involved.'

'Well let's put it another way, he's been badly used by both his friends and you,' *Bulmer says.*

'What villain has ever felt anything less than hard done by at the hands of the CID,' *Sneed explains.*

Bulmer dismisses that with an impatient gesture. 'Last week, on the 14th, you had another meeting with Detective Sergeant Feast, in The George, in Adam's Street. He asked you for help for Peter Rogers when he came to trial.'

Sneed says, 'Sounds like a conflict of interest to me, uncle.'

Bulmer says, 'But you being someone never to let an opportunity pass, agreed to enlist the help of Detective Superintendent Stern, who was also on the case. You said it would cost £2,500.'

'Superintendent Stern? This is fucking nonsense,' *Sneed says, these details getting to him.*

'When DS Feast complained that the price was too steep, you said it was because of them other cunts. Superintendent Stern had to be involved, and would want the lion's share,' *Bulmer says.*

'You've got to give it a go. But none of this is worth a rub,' *Sneed points out.* 'Using agent provocateurs to draw up a crime where ordinarily none exists.'

'But wait a minute, you've been doing that throughout your career, chief inspector' *DCS Bulmer says.*

'With straight villains. They have to be put away,' *Sneed justifies.* 'But here we're talking about allegations of police corruption. The ground rules are different.'

'No one's informed us of that,' *DCS Bulmer says.*

'I can't see the DPP taking the same line,' *Sneed says.* 'Then I suppose he's a little more sophisticated.'

'You keep invoking the DPP as if he is some personal talisman,' *Bulmer says.* 'He works just as well for me. Like everyone else, he wants corruption stamped out.'

'That's something we all want,' *Sneed says.*

DCS Bulmer looks at him. 'Subsequent to your meeting with DS Feast you approached Superintendent Stern to ask help for Rogers, saying it would be worth two thousand pounds to him.'

'Harry Stern told you that?' *Sneed says, believing that he's ahead of the game.*

'He's agreed to go into the witness box,' *DCS Bulmer said.* 'As distasteful as he'd find giving evidence against a fellow officer.'

'I'd say Harry Stern would find perjury more distasteful,' *Sneed says.* 'Seeing that he's about the straightest detective I know. I think you'd better give me back my belt and laces. Either get on your bikes or bring your witnesses into court.'

'It's not altogether that simple chief inspector,' *Bulmer tells him.* 'We could go into court with you. A conviction would look very nice, having such a high ranking detective. But we want more, because we know there is more, and we know you're the key to it.'

'Ballocks! You've got fuck all; you'll get fuck all,' *Sneed says, on a worried note now.* 'You might get me to court, but that's about as far as it'll go. You'll just make a cunt of yourself.'

'There are witnesses prepared to give evidence against you,' *DCS Bulmer informs him.*

'Corrupt detectives who've had a gun put to their heads, you mean,' *Sneed says.* 'Villains with a vested interest in discrediting a good thief-taker.'

'There are the tape recordings of your conversations with DS Feast. They'll go down a treat with any jury,' *Bulmer says.*

'No way will the court admit those in evidence,' *Sneed argues.*

'You're underestimating how important this investigation is,' *Bulmer tells him.* 'There is need to restore public confidence in the police. What better way is there than putting all the corrupt policemen on trial? Special guidelines are being drawn up for dealing with these cases.'

'I don't give a fart what guidelines are drawn up. The fact is those tapes corroborate fuck all.' *Sneed waits a moment, watching the man.* 'If you really want to know what was going on at those meetings with Lenny Feast I'll tell you. On two occasions I'd been approached by a corrupt policeman, DS Feast as it happens. He was seeking help for villains awaiting trial. All I was doing was collecting evidence to take to the rubber heels,' *he explains.*

'Ah. I suppose it's worth a try, Terry,' *DCS Bulmer says.*

'It's in my diary uncle,' *Sneed says, coolly confident.* 'I don't go to such meetings without putting it in my diary. Otherwise you leave yourself on offer.'

'We have a very pretty piece of corroborative evidence, Terry,' *Bulmer says in a friendly way.* 'The fifteen hundred pounds which Feast gave you in that pub and which Chief Inspector Humpfress found in your possession when he searched you. All the notes were marked.' *He opens the folder to reveal the money.* 'You're experienced enough to know that this will substantiate everything that's on the tapes.'

Sneed feels the bite of the steel trap against his leg.

'You dirty, no-good cunts!' *he says.*

'It's the job we have to do, Terry,' *DCS Bulmer says.* 'So let's get down to business.'

There's a pause.

'How about that statement now?' *DCS Bulmer asks.*

'I want to talk to my boss, Commander Wiseman,' *Sneed says in a slight state of shock.*

'Not before you talk to us,' *Bulmer advises him.*

Sneed shakes his head in dismay. 'You've probably pulled more fucking stokes than me. Fuck it,' *resigning himself to the prospect.* 'You get Commander Wiseman down to see me, otherwise I don't talk to no one but my brief.'

DCS Bulmer considers that, then nods. He glances at his watch. 'Put him back in his cell, get him a bit of lunch. I'll have a word with Commander Wiseman. I think you'll see what fair-minded men we are, Terry.'

Sneed rises clutching his trousers. He picks up a bundle of money and considers it. 'Yeah, I'd say you were very fair, uncle,' *he says ironically.*

Sneed goes out with DS Preece.

Darkness.

ACT TWO

One

Sneed is brought into an interview room at the police station by DS Preece. He has his belt back, and is threading it around the belt loops on his trousers. He is still in the same clothes.

DC Horn brings in an armful of files, which he puts on the desk, then goes.

'Looks like it's going to be another busy day,' *Sneed observes.*

'Looks that way,' *DS Preece says, laying out the folders.*

'What d'you get out of this?' *Sneed asks.* 'I suppose it gives you a hard on, does it, nicking other policemen?

'I can't say as I've thought about it, sir,' *Preece says.* 'One bad lad is much the same as another. Some you feel more pleased about putting away.'

'What about when it means fitting them?' *Sneed challenges.* 'You have a conscience about that?'

'I don't know anything about it, sir,' *Preece says.*

'No You're just doing your job, pal,' *Sneed says.*

Sneed considers him, then turns away. He casually flicks open one of the folders on the table. 'Denis Rawlings!' *he says reading the name, a bit surprised.* 'What's this doing here? We had a right result with him. He got fifteen years.'

'We're looking into everything that has brought about a complaint, sir,' *Preece tells him.*

'Denny Rawlings complained? *Sneed is amazed.* 'Fucking cheek!'

'I think his solicitor did, sir – when he heard you were arrested. He's claiming you manufactured the evidence,' *Preece explains.*

'Oh well, that's standard,' *Sneed says.* 'It's the fucking same, whenever a villain's nicked. The first thing he screams is a fit-up.' *He stops abruptly when DS Preece looks at him, realising he has done the same thing.*

'Not me, pal. I really am being fitted up on this one,' *he says and turns away.*

DC Horn comes in with more folders. 'Can you hang on here now, Roy,' *DS Preece says.* 'I've got a couple of witnesses to chase up.'

He goes out.

DCI Humpfress comes into the room with DCS Bulmer. Both have more folders.

'Morning, Terry,' *DCS Bulmer says.* 'Sleep all right?'

'Wonderful – there was a wino in the next cell retching his heart out.'

'We've been doing our homework,' – *referring to the folders.* 'You've your belt and laces back. Good. Everything else all right?'

'Oh terrific. S'like Butlins,' *Sneed says.* 'Mind you, be nice to have a Redcoat to fuck in my cell.'

'That sort of facility is only given to prisoners who are particularly helpful.'

'Supergrasses,' *Sneed says.* 'I need a shower and a change of clothes. S'been three days now. S'fucking liberty.'

'The sooner we get done the sooner you shower and change,' *Bulmer offers.*

'What about Commander Wiseman?' *Sneed asks.* 'I thought you were getting him down here to see me. How often do I have to ask?'

DCS Bulmer shakes his head. 'That's not on. Your boss has disowned you.'

'What d'you mean, disowned me?' *Sneed is puzzled.* 'Is that what he said?'

'He's not interested in becoming caught up in your troubles, Terry,' *the DCS tells him.*

'Oh that's a nice cunt.' *Sneed says.*

'Well what could he do for you – in view of the evidence?' *Bulmer says.* 'I'm the only one with any control over what help you might get now.'

'What do you want? I'm not putting my hands up,' *Sneed tells them.*

'You could do worse,' *Bulmer says.*

'Are you sure I got a knock back from Commander Wiseman?' *Sneed is disbelieving.*

DCS Bulmer considers him for a moment. 'Do you want to call him yourself? As of now you can't make your position worse. You can only improve it, Terry. The DPP is interested in a deal.'

'You want the names of a few detectives at it?' *Sneed says.*

'That would help our investigation, and help you,' *Bulmer says.*

'Just how exactly will it help me?' *Sneed wants to know.*

'Something could be worked out,' *Bulmer tells him.*

'Fuck off,' *scoffs Sneed.* 'I've broken too many promises to villains myself to have any faith in a policeman's word.'

'Not me, Terry,' *Bulmer tells him.* 'This would be down to the DPP – he's an honourable man. He'd be prepared to offer some arrangement whereby you quietly retire.'

'That's fifteen years' work out the window,' *Sneed says.*

'The alternative could be fifteen years in prison,' *Bulmer points out.*

Sneed says, 'I'd sooner take my chances in court.'

'Sir Trevor Rump believes there's sufficient evidence to successfully prosecute,' *DCS Bulmer tells him.* 'As for your record what we've found will only add nails to the coffin. Villains are crawling out of the woodwork to complain. You'd be a fool to pass up any offer of help.'

'Especially as you have no senior officer to speak for you,' *DCI Humpfress puts in. He's put out that his boss is taking over so much.*

'Yes, that's something any jury's bound to wonder about,' *DCS Bulmer says.*

'Why are senior officers refusing to speak for you?' *DCI Humpfress asks.* 'Think about it.'

'They're no-good fucking slags, is why,' *Sneed says in a fit of pique.*

'Commander Wiseman is sensibly looking after his own interests,' *Bulmer says.* 'He's assessed the evidence and wisely decided there's no point involving himself. Looking after number one, that's what he's doing.'

'Well you'd better see that cunt again and tell him if I'm nicked I'll take as many with me as I can,' *Sneed threatens.*

'That's the spirit, Terry,' *DCS Bulmer encourages.* 'The sort of cooperation we like to hear. The more you name, the better the deal you eventually get.'

'I'll tell you something, if I did start naming names,' *Sneed threatens,* 'I'd name so many fucking detectives at it, there won't be a CID left in London.' *Sneed paces.* 'Go and see Commander Wiseman again, tell him either he talks to me, or I talk to you.'

'I know what his reaction will be, Terry,' *Bulmer advises.* 'You can't hurt him personally.'

'You put it to him,' *Sneed says.* 'See how *he* likes a fucking gun to his head.'

Bulmer agrees with a shrug. 'I'll have another word with him, see if he'll change his mind. I'll leave you to it, Brian,' *he says to DCI Humpfress. He considers Sneed, then goes out.*

'We'd like to ask some questions about some of your more recent cases,' *Humpfress says.*

'Ask what you like, uncle,' *Sneed says.*

'Jimmy Mitchell – you arrested him for robbing a Securicor van out at Heathrow,' *Humpfress says.*

'He's on remand. He's not claiming he was fitted, for fucksake,' *Sneed says.*

'No,' *DCI Humpfress says.* 'He admits his involvement. But what he is saying is that you took money off his partners to keep him in the frame and them out of it.'

'What's his problem?' *Sneed asks, leaving DCI Humpfress puzzled.* 'All he's got to do is convince the jury when he goes up the steps. Should be easy enough.'

'I wouldn't have thought it difficult,' *Humpfress says.* 'After all we've arrested his partners, and they're saying the same thing. Not only that, they're saying that you put them on to the job in the first place.'

'Fuck I, you have been busy,' *Sneed says a little dismayed.* 'They say how much I s'pose to have earnt?'

'£16,000 was mentioned,' *DCI Humpfress says.*

'Would've been a right good earner,' *Sneed says.* 'A few like that would be handy.'

'You weren't seeing yourself short,' *Humpfress says, referring to a file.* 'Barry Tucker gave you £10,000 from a security truck robbery in Newham.' *He picks up another folder.* 'A bank robbery in Fulham, for which only one person was arrested – netted you £11,000.' *He looks at Sneed a little amazed.* 'What do you do with all this money?'

'Well if I had it and had invested it,' *Sneed says,* 'I'd be a mug not to take that deal and retire.'

'Let me tell you something, chief inspector,' *Humpfress says* 'despite my boss coming in here and making all kinds of promises to you, no one's going to let you quietly retire. This operation has been sixteen months of hard work and almost £2 million of public money, that's what the brass have to justify. They're going to nail you anyway they can.'

'Why are you telling me all this?' *Sneed asks.*

'Because I'm a decent, fairminded policeman. I don't want to see even you make a fool of yourself,' *DCI Humpfress says.*

Sneed considers this. Then says, 'I'll take my chances, uncle.'

'Your record says you're academically very bright. But at the moment you're being very stupid. You have no chance, Terry, believe me.' *He grasps Sneed's hands to earnestly make his point.* 'Too many people are willing to give evidence against you. You'll have to talk to someone sooner or later. Talk to me.'

'What's in that for me – sweet FA. Where's the value?' *Sneed wants to know.*

'Do you ever go to church, Terry?' *DCI Humpfress asks.* 'It's sometimes good to unburden yourself.'

'I got married in church – can't say that was much to recommend it,' *Sneed says.* 'I had no need to go again – they didn't do divorces.'

'I go regularly, myself,' *Humpfress says.* 'To a Methodist chapel in Salisbury.'

'What do you pray for, a nice few collars?' *Sneed asks.*

'Whenever I've done anything wrong I find it a great relief to talk to someone who's prepared to listen,' *DCI Humpfress says.*

'You really go in and tell Him about all your earners?' *Sneed asks.*

'You can talk to Him about anything,'

Humpfress advises him.

'That's right, with no prospect of being nicked,' *Sneed points out.* 'Myself, I've never felt any need. If it's all the same to you, I'll have a word with Commander Wiseman.'

'You're convinced he's going to help?' *DCI Humpfress says.*

'Well he ought to,' *Sneed says,* 'half the fucking time he's convinced he's God.'

DCI Humpfress nods. He's disappointed, 'Take him back to his cell, Roy,' *he says to DC Horn, as he gathers up the folders.*

'I'll tell you what, uncle', *Sneed says as he starts out with Horn.* 'If I do eventually have to talk to anyone, I'd just as soon it were you.'

He goes, followed by Humpfress.

Two

'Terry Sneed. I must confess to being amazed he has got himself into this sort of mess,' *Commander Wiseman says as he comes along the corridor with DCS Bulmer. They stop at the drinks vending machine. He puts a coin in.* 'I always believed Sneed to be a first rate thief-taker. His methods may sometimes have been a little swift, but it's the results that matter.'

'Some of those results are now being reassessed, commander,' *DCS Bulmer says.* 'There are some behind bars for villainy they didn't do.'

'I'm not surprised. A person can't be that interested in locking people away without one or two of the wrong 'uns go. Just so long as no one is suggesting we release those villains Sneed put away. D'you want hot chocolate?' *he offers, taking the cup.* 'I can't hold to my diet.' *He is largish, bald, in his early 50s, overweight. Commander Wiseman is continually dieting, and always breaking diet and eating double to make up for the loss, so tends to go up and down like a leaky tyre. As a result his clothes don't fit him very well.*

'I'll get coffee,' *DCS Bulmer says, producing his own 5p.*

'That's the danger with this sort of enquiry,' *Commander Wiseman continues.* 'If we're not careful bent lawyers will be queuing up to complain that clients were convicted as a result of perjured evidence.'

'They could have a point, commander,' *DCS Bulmer says.*

'There's no way the attorney general can allow such a notion to get airborne,' *Wiseman says.* 'I can't see that it makes much difference how villains are convicted.' *He sips some hot chocolate.* 'There is absolutely no doubt about Sneed's involvement?'

'Things look fairly bleak,' *DCS Bulmer says.*

'He's still not made a statement?' *Commander Wiseman asks.*

DCS Bulmer shakes his head. 'I don't suppose you've changed your mind about having a word?'

'I can't see that I want to get involved,' *Wiseman says.* 'I've always backed my officers fully, they know my position regarding private enterprise. DCI Sneed included.'

'Is that what I'm to tell him, commander?' *DCS Bulmer asks.*

'I think I've made myself clear,' *Wiseman says.* 'I'm not speaking for him or any other corrupt policeman. Not to your lot, the assistant commissioner or anyone else. That's my final word. I'm not going to be dragged into this bloody mess. He knows the price of getting caught. The bloody fool. It's such a waste.'

'He has of course been issuing all sorts of silly threats. He said he isn't prepared to stand on his own in the frame,' *DCS Bulmer informs him cautiously.* 'In that event he plans to take as many with him as he can. He threatens to involve so many detectives that there'd hardly be a CID left in London.'

'He said that?' *Wiseman says, changing tack as he becomes more worried.* 'Did he mention any rank?'

'It wasn't a serious threat, I felt,' *Bulmer says, playing the man on a line.* 'Oh I don't doubt he knows one or two other corrupt policemen. Be as well to pull them in.'

'I don't know how he imagines I can help him,' *Wiseman says.*

'I can't see why you'd want to.'

'I want to see every last vestige of corruption stamped out,' *Commander Wiseman*

continues, shifting ground some more.
'What possible point could there be in my seeing him in cells?'

'Well I can understand your having no inclination to help Chief Inspector Sneed. But the thing is, sir,' *Bulmer says,* 'he's very hostile towards the policemen on Operation Bad Apple. This isn't helping us in our interviews.'

'I don't imagine he'd exactly consider his arrest a fair cop!' *Commander Wiseman says.*

'I was thinking, commander, he might say something to you, that he won't to us.' *DCS Bulmer says.* 'If you were to agree to see him.'

'Yes, I suppose that is a possibility. You think I should see him?' *Wiseman asks.*

'It might help us, sir. If he does have any expectation of help from you, it would be as well to disillusion him,' *Bulmer tells him.*

'Then perhaps I should see him. Possibly I owe him that much.' *Wiseman considers this.* 'Yes, I will pop down and see him', *he says, looking at his watch.*

'That might help us,' *Bulmer is pleased.* 'I'll call up and advise them you're coming.'

'That might be best.'

They go off along the corridor together.

Three

Terry Sneed is brought into a new cell by a gaoler policeman. He brings with him a tray of lunch. He is still in his same clothes.

'What's wrong with the other cell?' *Sneed asks.*

'The plumber's going to fix the wc, sir,' *the gaoler says.* 'Stop it smelling.'

'Looks like another pisshole to me' *Sneed says.* 'I daresay the smell of disinfectant stops you tasting this.'

'I think you're having a visitor from the Yard, sir,' *the gaoler confides to him.* 'That's the reason for the clean cell.'

'Oh he'll be very impressed,' *Sneed says looking around the cell.*

The policeman goes.

Sneed picks at the food on his tray. Then he tries a mouthful of tea. None of it very appetising.

The gaoler reappears with Commander Wiseman.

'Oh, in the middle of lunch, Terry?' *Wiseman says in a friendly sort of way.*

'I haven't eaten shit like this since Hendon, guv,' *Sneed says.*

'The quality of the food is the least of your problems right now,' *Wiseman says.* 'Wait outside,' *he tells the uniform gaoler.*

'Yes, sir.' *He goes.*

Wiseman considers Sneed. 'This is a jolly fine mess, Terry. You're the one policeman I would have expected more from, to be perfectly honest.'

'To be perfectly honest, guv, I can't say I want a lecture right now. I'm more interested in what can be done,' *Sneed says.*

'I'm not sure there is anything,' *Wiseman tells him.* 'Not with the evidence there seems to be against you. Had a word with Assistant Commissioner Vyvyan, he thought it was a bit of a lost cause trying to help you in any way.'

'Oh I see,' *Sneed says,* 'I'm being offered the prick.' *He waits, anger and resentment running through him.* 'Well if I stay nicked,' *Sneed threatens.* 'I'll pull every cunt who's ever had sixpence into the frame.'

'I don't see any need for that attitude, Terry,' *Wiseman says.* 'This is not something you should take personally. You're simply a victim of the excess need to re-establish some sense of balance.'

'Well I won't be nicked on my own', *Sneed informs him.* 'I guarantee that.'

'Will you have enough evidence to involve lots of other detectives?'

'I'd say so,' *Sneed says.* 'You must know I couldn't be off that.'

Wiseman nods slowly. 'I do believe you could cause the Met a lot of damage. I suppose my reputation might suffer by implication.'

'You're being a bit optimistic, guv,' *Sneed says.* 'I can think of a dozen very senior officers who could be nicked straight off.'

'What sort of nonsense is this?' *Wiseman*

says, suddenly rattled. 'How senior are you talking about?'

'How senior do you want?' *Sneed says casually.* 'For a start, guv, there's yourself. Commander Burland, Assistant Commissioner Vyvyan, DCS Shaw, and DCS Markham. You all had money out of that payroll robbery. that's just one job.'

'That is fucking nonsense, Terry. I've never heard anything so ridiculous,' *Wiseman insists.*

Sneed nods, casually, almost enjoying this. 'That's standard. No one expects you to put your hand up. Both you and Commander Franklyn are having money out of the porn shops in Soho.'

'Be a man, son. Take what's coming to you like a man,' *Wiseman says, changing his tack.* 'Why try to drag everyone else down? No one's going to admire you for it.'

'Who the fuck wants to be admired?' *Sneed says.*

Wiseman cautions, 'All you'll succeed in doing is making a lot of enemies for yourself, Terry.'

'That's something I'll live with.'

'But you have friendship, trust, loyalty – that's what you're giving up,' *Wiseman says,* 'taking this narrow, self-seeking path.'

Sneed says, 'I thought I'd been one very cautious copper. More cautious than most. The mistake I made was underestimating them other cunts. But there's fuck all I can do about that now. All I can do is put on some pressure on, get what help I can.'

Wiseman says on an earnest note, 'You must know I'd be first to lend a hand to get you out of this mess if I could. But I'm not sure there can be any help, at this stage. This isn't the usual CIB2 investigation where I can simply pick up the phone and advise the officer in charge – a Met officer – what's in the best interest of both the service and his career. There's an awful lot of pressure on this investigation to succeed.'

'Fuck it! I don't mind it succeeding, guv,' *Sneed says.* 'Just so long as it does so without me in the frame. I think you'll have to have another talk to Assistant Commissioner Vyvyan.'

'Terry, Terry, I've talked to him.' *Wiseman is shaking his head doubtfully.* 'You don't seem to realise how solid their case against you is.'

'Do you remember when I nicked that architect, Laurence James? For corruption and perverting the course of justice,' *Sneed reflects.* 'Do you remember your advice over that case, guv: that it wasn't in the public interest he was nicked as James knew too much about too many people at it, in key places? Including the minister for Trade and Industry of the day, and the minister for the Environment, not to mention the minister for Housing.'

'The case was very delicate,' *Wiseman recalls.* 'One likely to embarrass the government.'

'No doubt. But what happened? We managed to lose all the evidence.'

'It went into the paper shredder on the seventeenth floor, much to everyone's relief,' *Wiseman says.*

'But not before it went into the xeroxing machine on the fourth floor,' *Sneed says.*

'You made a copy of that file?' *Wiseman is alarmed.*

'Every last page. The thing is, guv, that's just one ramp. I've got the dates; the amounts, the bodies involved with every bit of business we ever did,' *Sneed tells him.*

'Committed to paper? Is that what you're saying?'

'Everything you and I ever bent. The same with everyone else I did business with.'

This brings a remarkable change of attitude in Commander Wiseman. He sinks onto the cot bed breathlessly, as if punched in the stomach.

'Don't worry,' *Sneed says.* 'The only way this is going to fall into the hands of those other cunts is if by some remote chance all that evidence against me couldn't somehow be lost.'

'You're a first rate detective, Terry,' *Wiseman says after a moment.* 'Your record is excellent. The Met can't afford to lose such officers.' *He considers this.* 'I'll speak to the assistant commissioner again – have him reassess the evidence, reconsider whether the charges are worth proceeding with. I somehow doubt that they are, myself. Never thought so, to be quite candid. These country detectives are trying a little too hard.'

'About right, guv,' *Sneed concedes.*

'Good. Well, I'm glad we had this chat, Terry.' *He rises, having recovered himself.* 'Anything you need? Any little thing to make life more bearable?' *Wiseman offers.*

'A shower and a change of clothes would be handy,' *Sneed says.* 'I'm beginning to smell worse than this peter. Oi!' *he calls to the gaoler.*

'Leave it to me,' *Wiseman says. He pauses awkwardly.* 'Right. I'll be in touch, Terry.'

'Good luck, guv.' *Sneed says.*

The uniformed gaoler comes in. 'All through, sir?' *he says to Wiseman, who proceeds him out.* 'You can go back to the other cell now, sir,' *he says to Sneed.*

'What is this a get-up?' *Sneed says.*

'The plumber's fixed the lavatory,' *the gaoler tells him.*

'About right,' *Sneed says.*

He goes out, followed by the gaoler.

Four

'Before we proceed any further, Tony' *Assistant Chief Constable Leeper says, coming into his office with a folder and a tape recording and sitting at his desk.* 'The question we must seriously consider is this, has DCI Sneed hard evidence against these senior officers he's named here (*indicating the tape*) or is he clutching at straws? Personally I'm inclined to think this is going to turn into an enormous hoax, with us ending up with eggs on our faces.'

'In some ways I'd like to believe that, Alan,' *DCS Tony Bulmer says,* 'but it's not a banker's bet.'

'They didn't know you were wiring that cell?' *Leeper asks.*

'Hardly,' *Bulmer says.*

'But it's scarcely credible,' *Assistant Chief Constable Leeper argues,* 'that those officers he mentioned to Commander Wiseman could be so venal.' *He turns up the transcription of the tape.* 'He actually said Assistant Commissioner Vyvyan took money from that payroll robbery. No senior Met officer has supported our investigation more consistently.'

'There have been whispers about Commander Wiseman,' *DCS Bulmer suggests.* 'Mostly from the informers we have in police cells. You can't challenge commanders on something like that. Not without risking making a fool of yourself. But Sneed's evidence is a different matter entirely.'

'We are talking about the most senior officers in the Met,' *Leeper says, still finding this difficult to comprehend.* 'If Assistant Commissioner Vyvyan can be implicated like this, then why not the commissioner himself?'

'That would be a turn up for the book,' *DCS Bulmer says.* 'Why not?'

'It's ridiculous,' *the assistant chief constable says.* 'Senior policemen don't carry on in such a manner. There's no doubt that corruption is widespread, but fortunately it's confined to the lower ranks.'

'They were all lower ranks at one time,' *Bulmer points out.*

'So were we, Tony,' *Leeper says.*

'There's an argument for the theory that corruption starts at the top, not the bottom,' *DCS Bulmer says.*

'I'm not competent to pontificate on that,' *Leeper says.* 'There was no catalogue of evidence against senior officers found when you searched Sneed's flat.'

'Doesn't mean too much, Alan,' *Bulmer says.* 'There wasn't a single thing there that shouldn't have been. I mean most of us have something we can't account for, even if it's only a hotel spoon. But not Sneed.'

'Sure; sure; sure,' *Leeper interjects throughout.* 'Sure . . .'

'He's an extremely cautious man,' *DCS Bulmer says.* 'I wouldn't expect such evidence to be lying around his home. It wouldn't be worthy of him.'

'Well I could be wrong, Tony,' *Assistant Chief Constable Leeper says grudgingly.* 'I sometimes pray that I am wrong. But I think Sneed's as high as we'll go. However, what I'm sure he does know is how widespread the network of corruption below him is. If we can get stuck into that lot, it'll be a good job.'

'We'll have those out as well,' *Bulmer says.* 'But I don't accept that Sneed is where the corruption stops.'

'I'll need an awful lot of convincing before I approach the DPP. Or interview Commander Wiseman,' *Leeper says.*

'All we have to do is break Sneed,' *DCS Bulmer says.* 'I've a notion how I might do it.' *He retrieves the transcript from the desk.* 'Have you finished with this transcript?'

'Yes,' *Leeper says, giving his approval.* 'I might just have a word with Assistant Commissioner Vyvyan, unofficially.' *He picks up the tape.*

'Do you think that's wise at this stage, Alan?' *Bulmer asks.*

'Damn it, Tony', *Leeper responds angrily in his confusion.* 'He's tipped as the next commissioner. I think we must play fair by these officers.'

'I see,' *DCS Bulmer says resignedly.*

They both go out.

Five

DCI Terry Sneed precedes DCI Humpfress into an interview room, the latter bringing a number of files, which he puts on the table. Sneed is still in his same clothes.

'Is the DCS not joining us?' *Sneed asks.*

'He'll be along shortly,' *DCI Humpfress replies a little briskly.* 'Would you say I've treated you fairly?'

Sneed looks at him a moment. 'As well as could be expected.'

'Then why don't you play fair by me?' *Humpfress says.* 'Why don't you give me a statement, before the super' gets here.'

'That would help you out would it?' *Sneed asks, as if considering the notion.*

Humpfress says, 'It wouldn't do me any harm at all to be the one to crack this case. I've done most of the work.'

'That's always the same. You do all the graft, then you have your governor steam in and take the credit,' *Sneed agrees.*

'Well how about it?' *Humpfress asks.* 'We could get it wrapped up quite quickly.'

'Are you all right, Terry?' *DCS Bulmer asks as he comes into the interview room.* 'Getting everything you want?'

'I'm not getting my liberty,' *Sneed says.*

'To be frank that's becoming about as remote as the yeti,' *Bulmer tells him.*

'So's that fucking shower and change of clothes I was promised five days ago,' *Sneed says dismissively, sniffing himself in disgust.* 'I couldn't even pull a policewoman smelling like this.'

'Oh didn't Commander Wiseman fix that up?' *DCS Bulmer says.* 'I thought that was the point of his visit.'

Sneed looks askance, some inkling of what might have happened in that cell dawning on him.

'Anything you need?' *Bulmer says, reading from the transcript he has brought with him.* 'Any little thing to make life more bearable? A shower or a change of clothes would be handy – should be 'and', I think, not 'or'. The standard of police typing's terrible,' *Bulmer comments.* 'Your governor must've forgotten you, Terry. Then I don't doubt he's got more important things on his mind. Like how to shake himself clear of that payroll robbery. I daresay he's closeted with Assistant Commissioner Vyvyan and Commander Burland.'

'You dirty, snaky cunt,' *Sneed says as the truth becomes irrefutable to him.* 'I stood the fucking prick over that change of cell.'

'I wasn't hopeful about getting anything as good as this (*transcript*) from the wire in the cell,' *DCS Bulmer tells him.*

'I must be getting as silly as a fucking goat,' *Sneed says.*

'Even the most cunning detectives have off days,' *Bulmer says, mocking him.* 'I think it's time we got down to some hard trading Terry.'

Sneed doesn't respond.

'If you're pinning hopes on Commander Wiseman, forget it,' *Bulmer tells him.* 'Right now his only concern is how to get himself clear. It's save-yourself-time. I'm the only one who can save *you*, Terry, do some trading with the DPP on your behalf.'

Sneed looks at DCI Humpfress, remembering what he said about his boss's promises. 'That sounds like ballocks to me. That was my game, promising villains the earth.'

'Well isn't that a chance you'll have to take,' *DCS Bulmer says.*

There is a pause while Sneed considers this.

'Sit down, Terry. Let's have that natter,' *Bulmer invites.*

Still Sneed hesitates. Finally he resigns himself to the prospect. 'Oh fuck it, and all them slags,' *he says.* 'They can't say I didn't warn them.'

'Sit down, Terry,' *Bulmer says with a friendly smile.* 'Now do you want to write your own statement, or do you want us to write down what you say for you to sign?'

'We'd better get something sorted from the off, uncle,' *Sneed says, taking a chair.* 'What I'm prepared to give you is a lot of names and details – if I get some help, that'll be handy. What you do is then up to you, but I'm not signing a statement.'

'That's no problem', *Bulmer says.* 'Get Sergeant Preece in here to take down the details, as well, Brian.'

DCI Humpfress goes quickly out.

'What made you change your mind, Terry?' *DCS Bulmer asks.*

'Does it matter?' *Sneed wants to know.*

'Professional pride, I suppose,' *Bulmer says. He waits.*

'When I started as a young detective,' *Sneed says,* 'the first DS I worked with gave me a piece of advice about taking earners or fitting anyone. He said if it ever came on top and you got nicked, always deny it and go on denying it, even if you're bang to rights.'

'So why have you decided to cough?' *Bulmer asks, puzzled.*

'Well I very soon realised when I passed that same advice on to other detectives,' *Sneed says,* 'that it wasn't given for my sake but his. All the while I went on denying whatever was put to me, I couldn't involve him. It's the same with this little turnout. All the while the brass are kept out of the frame, they're not going to do very much. So I've nothing to lose by seeing how they shape up.'

'Just for the record, Terry,' *Bulmer says when Humpfress returns with Preece and a ream of paper,* 'you're not giving this information as the result of duress, or any promise we made you?'

'Cor, how could you threaten me,' *Sneed says sarcastically.*

'Right, in your own words then, Terry,' *Bulmer says.*

Sneed hesitates on the precipice before throwing himself off. 'You got some of the names of the firm from the wire you stuck in the cell,' *Sneed says.* 'There's always been a firm within a firm in the CID.'

All three of the detectives grouped around the table with him are writing, though DCS Bulmer only notes odd names.

'You heard me mention the assistant commissioner, well, Peter Vyvyan's been at it ever since he was chief superintendent on Division. I'd say he was at it long before that,' *Sneed says.*

'What d'you know of his activities on Division, Terry?' *Bulmer asks.* 'We may as well fill in the gaps as we go.'

'A thing I was directly involved with was a shipment of silver hijacked from a train at Barking. Two bodies were put up. One was called Foot, I can't remember the other guy. Foot was well fitted, partly as a favour to some villains running that manor at the time. Foot and his partner had been taking liberties.'

'How much did Assistant Commissioner Vyvyan receive?' *Bulmer asks.*

'About a grand, I think. That was the going rate for a DCS in those days. I mean, ten years ago, a DS would cop fifty quid and think he'd had a good earner. Anyone tried bunging a DS a fifty now, he'd tell them to fuck off. When Peter Vyvyan became responsible for porn and vice, that was the worst bit of news Soho had had since the Krays. Then he really came into his own. He established the payment system. I don't think there was anyone dabbling who wasn't weighing on,' *Sneed reflects.* 'Mind you, he upset a few. That's how Ron Drake came to be nicked. I mean, the Squad which Drake was running was fuck all to do with Soho. But even so, Commander Drake thought he was entitled to earn a few quid there. Peter Vyvyan decided otherwise. The upshot was that Drake was stuck up over a visit he made to Steenie Collins's villa in Spain. Vyvyan made the information available to the *Sunday Mirror,* and the Rubber Heels nicked Drake. Ernie Wiseman who was my boss at West End Central got his job and things were as sweet as a nut. Everyone got their whack.'

'Who did the collecting and sharing out, Terry?' *Bulmer asked.*

'Me, a DI called Michael Bryant and a DC called Frank Bedsted. I think Peter Vyvyan must have seen the writing on the wall because not long after he got made deputy assistant commissioner there was that awful fucking row over corruption in the Porn Squad; a few detectives were nicked, then responsibility for porn got handed over to the uniform branch. Who found himself sitting at the head of it again? Deputy Assistant Commissioner Vyvyan. So it was more or less business as usual.'

'Are you speculating on that,' *Bulmer asks,* 'or do you know this for a fact, Terry?'

'Well you must have had more than enough complaints from dealers in Soho,' *Sneed says.* 'I was well active in the Squad by this time so I wasn't doing the collecting. But if you pull Superintendent Ron Monday of C1, he'll have all the details. He's only got about a year to go before he retires. He's shitting himself in case anything like this happens to prevent that, so he won't be hard to crack. Peter Vyvyan's actually a very good copper. A lot of them up there get out of touch. Not only does he know how to organise the practical side of coppering, putting policy into effect, he knows how to formulate that policy. Here in the Met there's a lot of lobbying for increased police powers. What Peter Vyvyan has done is formulated policy to achieve that. His was the master-stroke to pile pressure on the blacks in the most volatile areas. That way you increase racial tension, which brings about more and more conflict on the streets. This acts as an indicator to the breakdown of law and order. That's something the public firmly believes is happening.'

'That wasn't such a masterstroke after all,' *DCS Bulmer says,* 'as it turned out.'

'Well Scarman did give us a bit of a spanking – he was well out of fucking order, but when the home secretary eventually asks

Parliament to increase police powers, what MP would vote against it as week after week there are reports in the press of street riots, pictures of policemen with bloody heads. You can't deny that's a brilliant stroke by Peter Vyvyan,' *Sneed says.*

'Brilliant?' *DCI Humpfress says.*

Bulmer looks at him a little. 'Can we have some details of the wrong-doing he's been up to?' *he asks.*

'His strokes,' *Sneed says.* 'Yes, well s'not something I carry in my head. Everything I was involved in, where it affected someone else, I noted down and filed it for future reference.'

'You should join CIB2, Terry. I daresay they would like to have recruited you,' *Bulmer observes.* 'Tell us about the payroll robbery.'

'It was a straightforward bit of business,' *Sneed says.* 'The villain who plotted it up wanted to know if I could go into anyone at the City police. I know more than enough CID in there who are at it, but I thought it would be good policy to bring in Commander Wiseman. He did the business with Chief Superintendent Taber. They both copped seven grand apiece. I had four. A couple of DIs copped four. There was about a dozen on the Squad who had a grand, and more than a dozen over there who copped a grand apiece.'

'Did the robbers get anything?' *DCI Humpfress asks on a bitter note.*

'The blag came to about 170 grand,' *Sneed says.*

'How do you know all these sums were involved?' *Bulmer asks.*

'I acted as the gobee – I took the money around to everyone who was due a taste,' *Sneed says.*

'You said Assistant Commissioner Vyvyan was involved?' *Bulmer prompts.*

'He had five grand – which I delivered out to his house,' *Sneed says.*

'As a matter of interest, chief inspector,' *Bulmer asks* 'how many working policemen would you estimate to be involved in corruption?'

'That I personally know to be at it? Or who I could reasonably speculate about?' *Sneed asks, giving himself time to think.*

DCS Bulmer says, 'Indulge us with some speculation first.'

'I'd say we'd be talking about something like 95% of the CID. Depending how you're defining corruption,' *Sneed says.*

'There's only one way. Indictable activity,' *DCS Bulmer says.*

'It's never that straightforward it is? You must know yourself, Tony, that sometimes you have to be a bit swift if villains won't go any other way,' *Sneed says.* 'Strictly speaking you might say that is wrong, but it would have to be a right bastard who'd nick you for that.' *He waits.* 'It's still 95%. Policemen at it who I know personally, I'd say it was nearer to three hundred than two.'

'You have evidence on each of these?' *Bulmer asks, slightly incredulously.*

'These are policemen I know involved in major corruption,' *Sneed says.* 'I mean I haven't fucked around noting details of disciplinary matters, fiddled expenses or overtime. Mind you, if you catch one of them pulling those sort of strokes, you know it's a million he's gonna be susceptible to bigger things. I mean, let's face it everyone's at it nowadays. S'fact of life.'

'Presumably these three hundred corrupt policemen will know others that you don't know?' *DCI Humpfress says. He is still angry.*

'I'd be surprised if they didn't.' *Sneed laughs.* 'I told you you might regret nicking me.'

'You know what this means, don't you?' *DCS Bulmer says gravely.*

'I know,' *Sneed says.* 'The question is, do they know?'

'Commander Wiseman? Has he been involved in as many incidents of corruption as yourself?'

Sneed says, 'Could be he's had a lot more, after all, he's a lot older.'

'But has he had a piece of everything you've been involved in?' *DCS Bulmer asks.*

'Don't talk silly. You only involve the likes of Ernie Wiseman when he's useful. I mean, the kind of whack commanders look for, you'd be working for them the whole time.'

'Did either he or you ever do anything for nothing?' *DCI Humpfress asks.*

Sneed says, 'I've never known detectives do fuck all for nothing.'

'Some put in hundreds of hours of unpaid overtime on cases,' *DCI Humpfress says.*

Sneed looks at him.

'I'm talking about business, uncle,' *he says.*

'What corruption is Commander Burland involved with?' *DCS Bulmer asks.*

'There are a number of ramps he's had – one was helping a firm of car thieves specialising in Rovers and Jaguars and shipping them to the continent. They were nicked, but he saw to it the evidence disappeared,' *Sneed says.*

'What was the firm?' *Bulmer asks.*

'A lad called Eddie Roseman ran it. Still does as far as I know,' *Sneed says.*

'How was Burland involved in the newspaper payroll robbery?' *DCS Bulmer asks.*

'The stolen vehicles used on that came under his jurisdiction,' *Sneed says.* 'The idea was that they shouldn't be tied into the blaggers. Apart from the body who was being fitted for it.'

'How was that to be arranged?'

'The City detective who arrested Frank Tebbutt, – he was elected for that one, picked him up in one of the stolen cars for the blag. That way Tebbutt couldn't avoid having his finger prints all over it,' *Sneed explains.*

'Does Frank Tebbutt have any idea what happened?' *DCI Humpfress asks.*

'He's got to be a cunt if he doesn't,' *Sneed replies.* 'I mean, he's the only one waiting to go up the steps.'

'He's got to be a cunt anyway standing for that,' *DCI Humpfress says.* 'Although I suppose villains do have a big disadvantage. They don't expect that sort of behaviour from policemen.'

Sneed looks at him in disbelief. 'You've got to be a cunt, you believe that?'

DCI Humpfress thinks about this. 'Maybe it's to my credit after sixteen months of hearing filth like this about policemen.'

'Believe what you like, uncle,' *Sneed tells him.* 'It's results that count.'

There is an awkward pause.

'Has Eddie Roseman ever been interviewed?' *DCS Bulmer asks his DCI. He feels instinctively that he must support Humpfress, but doesn't wish to upset Sneed.*

'The name's not familiar, boss,' *DCI Humpfress says.* 'He could've been, in the early days.'

'Where is all this evidence you spoke of, Terry?' *DCS Bulmer asks.* 'It might be simpler if we were to take that as our starting point.'

'It's well safe,' *Sneed says.* 'But the thing is, what sort of help it's going to get me.'

'I'll be perfectly frank, Terry,' *DCS Bulmer says,* 'our assistant chief constable is reluctant to believe that high ranking policemen could be involved, not even on your say so. If you have evidence to corroborate all this – that's what the DPP will respond to.'

Sneed hesitates, 'I've got it. It's in a safe-deposit box.'

'That sounds like a safe place,' *Bulmer tells him.* 'Where's the key?'

'In another safe-deposit box, *Sneed says.*

'In the same bank?' *Bulmer asks.*

Sneed shakes his head.

'No, naturally not. And the key to that box?' *Bulmer says.*

'In a bank. I just call up and warn them when I want the key,' *Sneed explains.*

'It might be an idea if you phoned the bank now. We'll collect the key. Get the key from the second box, open the first and get all this evidence. Do you see any problems with that?'

'None that strike me,' *Sneed says.*

'Good. We'd better do that before the banks shut,' *he says looking at his watch as he rises.* 'Can you arrange to see Tebbutt in Brixton, Brian? And pick up Roseman and his firm. Come on, Terry.'

They all go out at a brisk pace.

Darkness.

Six

Assistant Chief Constable Leeper comes into Assistant Commissioner Peter Vyvyan's office and waits. The loo en suite is flushed and Peter Vyvyan comes with a thick report which Leeper has sent him.

'Ah, morning, Leeper,' *Vyvyan says, trying to assert his authority.* 'This makes terrifying reading.' *He indicates the report.*

'It is rather disturbing,' *Leeper confirms, embarrassed at this meeting.*

'Terrifying. Though I must congratulate you. Your detectives have been more active in this past fortnight,' *Vyvyan says.* 'Is chief Inspector Sneed still in police cells?'

'He's still assisting with our enquiries,' *Leeper says rather formally.*

'A dangerous man that, very dangerous,' *AC Vyvyan says ruefully.* 'He's like a wounded animal, trying to hurt anyone he can in order to reduce his own pain. Has the DPP seen this?' – *indicating the report.*

'I thought it only proper to approach you first, sir.' *Leeper's embarrassment is increasing.*

Seizing his one opportunity, AC Vyvyan says, 'Well you realise it's all fucking nonsense, don't you? Vindictive fucking nonsense at that. I always suspected Sneed was no good – he was too active. A detective can't be that active unless he's mad or totally corrupt, or both,' *he says.* 'I suppose this is his only possible line of defence. He is quite obviously stark staring fucking mad. He named two thirds of the CID strength of the Yard here, plus half of those in the divisions.'

'You are saying it's not true, sir?' *Assistant Chief Constable Leeper asks, with a sense of relief.*

'I don't say there's no single grain of truth in it,' *Vyvyan allows.* 'I can believe lower ranking detectives might have been tempted. That's why you lot are here. But trying to drag in senior officers is nonsense.'

'He seems to have made out a good case,' *Leeper says.* 'He's been very thorough.'

'Well if you choose to take the word of a self-confessed corrupt policeman, against my word,' *AC Vyvyan says, sounding very hurt.* 'Over the past months you haven't exactly shown yourself to be very bright,

Leeper, but if you want to make a complete ass of yourself, put that up to the DPP.'

Assistant Chief Constable Leeper nods ponderously. 'I know what we've been thought of here, and what we've been called, but we've been prepared to put up with that.' *He pauses.* 'Do you know Vera Smaller?'

Vyvyan gives him an uncertain look. 'I've lived with her for the last thirty years,' *he says.* 'That's my wife's maiden name.'

'I know. She holds a deposit account in that name with the Midland.' *he waits.* 'It has £68,000 in it.'

'My wife's a very careful budgeter,' *Vyvyan tries.*

Leeper is unmoved.

A sense of desperation floods AC Vyvyan as he feels the ground suddenly slipping from under him. 'You know I could have retired four years ago on half pension,' *he says, as if in mitigation.* 'There was a good job in the offing with Firestone. I was a fool not to have taken it, plenty of job security, long holidays, chance to travel, the wife wanted me to. It's hard to give up the life . . .' *He stops abruptly and looks at the assistant chief constable, realising that they are beyond solving the problem here.* 'You're a snaky cunt, Leeper, and no mistake. You'd better put that up to the commissioner. I can tell you now you won't be thanked.' *He pauses.* 'Look, I could have my resignation on his desk before he's read that.' *He waits, but when Leeper is unyielding, he changes tack completely.* 'But I'm fucked if I'll do *you* any favours. If you want to make a complete ass of yourself, go right ahead.'

There is a pause.

Assistant Chief Constable Leeper collects up his report.

Expecting Leeper to capitulate, AC Vyvyan's nerves are scraped raw at this point. He's about to extend his argument, but emits a small cry of distress instead and heads back into the loo.

Assistant Chief Constable Leeper waits in the office with his briefcase. After a moment the loo flushes and Commissioner Sir Denis Whites, comes into the office in uniform and carrying the report. He's a large man, slightly overweight.

'This is absolutely devastating,' *the commissioner says.* 'Absolutely bloody devastating. I've never read anything so disturbing. This'll ruin me, I can't continue in office once this gets out. It's absolutely ruinous.' *He plonks the fat report on the desk as if not wanting to be associated with it.* 'You had absolutely no authority to proceed as you have without consulting me or the DPP. Absolutely no authority.'

'With respect, commissioner,' *Assistant Chief Constable Leeper says deferentially.* 'My brief gave me the widest possible investigatory powers with regard to corruption within the Metropolitan Police. I believe I've stayed within that brief.'

'Yes, your brief did give you very wide ranging powers, Mr Leeper,' *the commissioner says.* 'Except when you started reaching these numbers, and such high ranking officers. Good god, you've caught people as high as this office.'

'Yes,' *Leeper says proudly.* 'At one time I didn't think we were going to get anywhere. Then we got that lucky break with Chief Inspector Sneed.'

'Lucky!' *the commissioner explodes with near-apoplexy.* 'It's not very lucky for me. It's not very lucky for the home secretary.' *He is becoming very agitated.* 'You've got fifty-four policemen in cells; I have resignations falling on my desk thicker than dandruff.'

'Some of the detectives interviewed did indicate they were going to resign, sir,' *Assistant Chief Constable Leeper confirms.* 'That would be too easy. I told them that their early resignations wouldn't exempt them from prosecution.'

'But there's a tradition in the Met of letting wrongdoers resign, their pensions intact,' *the commissioner points out.*

The assistant chief constable says, 'I was promised that wouldn't happen when I undertook this operation.'

'This absolutely won't do,' *the commissioner tells him.* 'We'll not have a CID left at this rate.' *He looks at the assistant chief constable who agrees.* 'Well, I don't intend to go down in police history as the commissioner responsible for that. The DPP will have to decide what to do. Excuse me.'

The commissioner hurries back into his lavatory.

The assistant chief constable waits.

After a moment Sir Trevor Rump, the DPP comes in, wearing a short camel hair coat with a velvet collar and a brown trilby. He's tall, very erect, in his late forties.

'Morning Leeper,' *he says openly.* 'Sir Denis not here?'

'Morning, sir,' *Leeper responds.* 'The commissioner's in the lavatory.'

'Ah, yes, my bowel motions became rather loose on reading your report,' *Sir Trevor says.* 'I must congratulate you, Leeper.'

'There's more to come, Sir Trevor,' *Leeper says.* 'A lot more.'

'One suspected corruption was quite extensive. But never did I imagine you would be this successful,' *Sir Trevor says.* 'I daresay there'll be a gong of some sort for you.'

'Thank you, sir,' *Leeper says.*

'Your star witness is still naming his confederates, is he?' *Sir Trevor asks, removing his coat.*

'The list seems endless,' *the assistant chief constable says, encouraged by this apparent support.*

'By the way, any chance he's mad? Wouldn't be the first policeman to become a raving loon from overwork,'' *Rump says.* 'There's no denying Sneed's a worker.'

'I'm not sufficiently competent to pontificate on his mental state, sir,' *Leeper says, uneasily now.* 'But the facts he's giving us are holding together.'

'I think we'd better have a psychiatrist see him anyway,' *Sir Trevor Rump says, following his own line of thought.* 'Could spare an awful lot of anguish in the long run.'

'He's not mad,' *Leeper says, sotto voce.*

'Ah, Denis', *Rump says as the commissioner emerges from his bathroom en suite.* 'I was just saying, the trick cyclist had better see Sneed. The fellow's obviously as mad as a March hare.'

'Oh absolutely balmy,' *the commissioner says, like a weight has just been lifted from his shoulders.* 'Yes, there can't be any doubt about him being bonkers. The sooner a psychiatrist confirms that the better. The pity is it's been left this late.' *The*

commissioner is smiling now. 'I think my secretary's put some coffee in the conference room. Assistant Commissioner Vyvyan and Commanders Wiseman and Burland will join us there.' *He offers them the door.*

'He's not mad,' *Assistant Chief Constable Leeper is saying as he quietly suffers a stroke.'*

They go out.

Seven

'Come in, chief inspector. I'm Dr. Bosé,' *Dr. Roald Bosé, a psychiatrist in his forties, says showing Sneed into his office.* 'Have a seat.' *He feels the coffee percolator on his desk.*

When Sneed goes and sits in the doctor's chair behind the desk, Bosé says, 'Or walk.'

'Walk?' *Sneed says.*

'About the office' *the doctor explains.* 'Some patients prefer to walk about while we talk.'

'Sitting's fine', *Sneed tells him.*

'I see.' *Dr. Bosé is disappointed at having lost his chair.* 'Would you like coffee? I don't have any milk.'

'Black's fine,' *Sneed says, leaning back in the chair at the desk.'*

'Is it? You don't mind black?' *Dr. Bosé takes two styrofoam cups from a long plastic roll, pours Sneed coffee. He offers it, expecting Sneed to reach for it, but finally puts it in front of him when the detective waits.* 'You know there's a move afoot to have you declared insane?'

'That sounds about right,' *Sneed says equitably.*

'How do you feel about that?' *Dr. Bosé asks.*

'Feel, what the fuck should I feel?' *Sneed wants to know.*

'Anger might not be unreasonable,' *the doctor says.* 'Do you feel angry?'

'Why the fuck should I?' *Sneed says.* 'These cunts're looking to survive, like everyone else. It's the sort of stroke I'd pull.

'Survival matters a great deal, does it?' *Dr. Bosé asks, walking about his office.*

'Talk like a cunt!' *Sneed chides.* 'If it didn't I wouldn't be fucking around here.'

'Faced with two options, on the one hand your being declared insane and allowed to resign; on the other prosecuted and sent to prison. Which would you choose.'

'What about the third option?' *Sneed asks.* 'Staying on in the job?'

'Do you think that's realistic?' *Dr. Bosé wants to know.*

'It could be done easily enough. Who the fuck will question it?' *Sneed says.*

'I thought that's what Operation Bad Apple was entirely about,' *Dr. Bosé says.* 'Questioning such wrong doing.'

'Things did get a bit out of hand,' *Sneed concedes.* 'About the only villains not getting a deal were the blacks picked up by the SPG.'

'Are the SPG untouchable?' *Dr. Bosé asks.*

'No. Most of the kids they do on sus haven't got any money,' *Sneed says.* 'The fact that there's been this extensive investigation is enough to satisfy most people. It won't make any difference whether six or six dozen detectives end up in the frame.'

'So you expect to be let go back to work, do you?' *Dr. Bosé asks.*
'If it can be done I daresay it will,' *Sneed says.* 'Unless someone decides I'm mad.'

'Do you think someone can do that regardless of whether you are or not?' *Dr Bosé asks.*

'I can decide whether someone's a villain or not,' *Sneed says.* 'All you'd need is another doctor to sign the Section.'

'How important is your work to you?' *Dr Bosé asks.*
'I'm a good detective,' *Sneed answers.*

'What's a good detective?' *Dr. Bosé wants to know.*

Sneed smiles. 'I claim more than my share of bodies.'

'No one questioning your methods?' *Dr. Bosé says.*

Sneed replies, 'Results are what everyone wants.'

'How do you feel when you achieve those results?' *Dr. Bosé says.*

Sneed looks at him for a long moment.

'Do you get a sense of achievement, satisfaction, power?' *the doctor continues.*

'What do you feel when you commit someone to the bin?' *Sneed replies.*

'Why do you always answer with a question?' *the doctor asks.*

'Because I'm used to asking questions,' *Sneed says.* 'I don't get a hard on when I get a villain sent down. Instead I think what a waste of human resource it is we're writing off in prison. I wonder what sort of society this is that requires the likes of me to pursue the likes of him.' *Sneed is really quite pleased with this 'right' answer.*

Dr. Bosé considers him a moment. 'Would you say you were sufficiently well remunerated?'

'Are you?' *Sneed asks.* 'The job's what you make of it. There's always some way to improve what's on the line. That's what everyone who works is doing.'

'You believe everyone fiddles?' *Dr. Bosé says.*

'That's what I'm paid to believe,' *Sneed replies.* 'I work hard at my job, I managed to acquire something nearer what I'm entitled to. I've got some property in Spain that can only go up in value. Some of the creature comforts. I wanna fuck someone, that's no problem; buy a few shares. I'm a survivor, that makes me a good copper. I've yet to nick a villain who's been anything but a loser. Successful villains I can count on the fingers of this hand, we never nick them. They're survivors.'

'You've been nicked, as you say,' *Dr. Bosé points out.*

'It's how you come out that matters,' *Sneed says.* 'I'll get some sort of result. Even if it means quietly retiring. That leaves me poncing around in my boat in Spain with a chick to swing on m' cock.'

'What sort of boat do you have?' *Dr. Bosé asks.*

'A 40 foot sloop, with a straight 16 MTU. It gives me about 800 horse,' *Sneed says casually.*

'That sounds really first rate,' *Dr. Bosé says.*

'What age is she?'

'The keel was laid in '76,' *Sneed says.* 'Solid mahogany.'

'There's so much trash on the market,' *Bosé says.* 'Plywood and paint. How often do you get out to Spain?'

'Twice a year for a holiday. I shoot across for a long weekend. S'cheap enough on the plane,' *Sneed explains.*

'Do you ever rent it out?' *Dr. Bosé asks.*

'Hadn't thought about it,' *Sneed says.* 'It doesn't eat fuck all – mooring fees are cheap enough. Did you fancy renting it?'

'It sounds very attractive. I have a small catamaran at Cowes. I don't manage to get down there as often as I'd like,' *Dr. Bosé says conversationally.*

'Maybe we could have a deal,' *Sneed says.* 'How long have you been into boats?'

'Ever since I was at medical school,' *the doctor says.* 'You?'

'Not long. An old guvnor of mine put me onto this as an investment. Boats are better bargains than houses at the moment. You can get a six berth ocean going yacht for £45,000. I figure it'll pick up again. Same with the houses I bought in Derry. At five hundred sovs a go, if they never settle their troubles, I'm still earning rent.'

'Are you optimistic about the troubles being solved out there?'

'People have got to live there whether they are or not,' *Sneed says.*

Dr. Bosé nods, as he considers the client. He's made up his mind about Terry Sneed.

'I have a colleague next door, a psychologist. I'd like it if you would do some tests with her,' *he says coming to the desk.* 'Then perhaps we can talk some more? How many berths does your boat have?' *the doctor asks.*

'Four doubles,' *Sneed tells him.*

'Oh that sounds ideal.' *Dr. Bosé is excited by this.* 'What sort of mooring fees do you have to pay? Mine are fucking astronomical.'

They go out.

Eight

Sir Trevor Rump, the DPP, appears on a golf course in a casual pullover and cravat, carrying a golf club. He's followed his ball, and Sir Denis Whites, the commissioner, is following him, carrying sets of clubs.

'Have you really never played golf, Denis?' *the DPP asks.*

'No,' *the commissioner says.* 'Nor have I ever done any caddying.'

The DPP says, 'It was the attorney general's idea. You know what Walter's like about Whitehall leaks. He doesn't want to be seen to be a party to anything resembling conspiracy to pervert the course of justice.'

'But our entire purpose is to see that justice is done,' *Sir Denis says.*

'Quite,' *the DPP says.* 'But then neither you or I rely on political favour for our jobs, Denis. We must allow the AG his caution. A pity about the psychiatric report on Sneed. Sweeping him under the carpet may have been the solution.'

'I suppose there is absolutely no point in going for a second opinion?' *the commissioner ventures.*

'I can't see the point myself,' the DPP says. 'Dr. Bosé is reckoned to be one of the best in his field. I'd imagine another psychiatrist would come to much the same conclusion about Sneed.'

'Oh, I didn't think they ever agreed about anything, psychiatrists,' *the commissioner says.*

'Then it would prove even more embarrassing if another opined that Sneed's aggressiveness, his highly developed acquisitiveness, his sharp sense of survival, made him as sane as you or I,' *the DPP says.*

At this point the commissioner grabs at his eye, misses what he's after, grabs twice at the air in front of him, then falls to the floor and scrabbles in the grass.

Sir Trevor Rump pulls back in alarm.

'Ah, is that my ball, Whites?' *Sir Walter Pursar, the attorney general, says as he appears with a golf club and cloth hat. He's an immaculately attired golfer; he's sixty and overweight.*

'My contact lens', *the commissioner says, holding it up.*

'Where's my fucking golf ball then?' *Sir Walter wants to know.*

'Here it is, Walter,' the DPP says, offering his own.

'That was your ball . . . ' *the commissioner says.*

'No it wasn't,' *the DPP says.* 'We were just discussing the psychiatric report on Sneed.'

'It's unfortunate that the doctors found the fellow so sane,' *Sir Walter says, shaping up with his putting iron to the DPP's ball.*

'As sane as any of us, I'm afraid, Walter,' *Sir Trevor Rump says.*

'If he could have been clapped in the loony bin, it may have shelved all sorts of problems,' *Sir Walter says.* 'I'm not sure that this state of affairs can continue much longer. If it does it's likely to cause the most godawful fucking stink.'

'It's certainly making the CID a great deal less effective,' *the commissioner says.*

'The home secretary's not happy. Charlie's under pressure from the cabinet to do something,' *the attorney general says.* 'What's the current position?'

'Leeper has actually stopped arresting policemen for the present,' *the commissioner explains.* 'But they are continuing to question those being held.'

'They have sufficient information to carry out more arrests?' *the AG asks.* 'Is that what you're saying?'

'I'm afraid so,' *Commissioner Whites says.* 'Those in police won't stop talking.'

'What's more, Walter,' *the DPP says,* 'on the sort of evidence that's being offered I'm bound to say there is a good chance of conviction.'

'This situation is ridiculous,' *the AG comments, stroking the air above his ball with his club.*

'It's absolutely absurd,' *the commissioner says,* 'An outside force should never have been allowed to investigate the Met.'

That stops all three of them. He's actually said what has been variously on their minds.

'Charlie wanted the image of the police cleaned up,' *the AG says.* 'Who am I to say that the Home Office went about it in the wrong way? The Government intends going to parliament quite soon to ask for increased police powers to deal with the extremists who are orchestrating this breakdown in law and order. The public need to be assured that those powers won't be abused in any way.'

'They absolutely won't, Walter,' *the commissioner says excitedly,* 'I give you my word.'

'I think perhaps we should urgently reappraise the means,' *the DPP says.*

'I was never in favour of an external investigation of this scope,' *the DPP says, moderating his position in the light of current opinion.* 'It never gave us implicit control. My deputies think a lot of it is out of order. They don't want to see these policemen prosecuted. We'll simply have to live with the media sniping about complaints being whitewashed.'

'That's a lot easier for you to live with,' *the commissioner says.* 'You know full well who gets blamed for all this corruption.'

'Well you have rather let things get out of hand, Denis,' *the DPP says.*

'If you'd only prosecute more effectively,' *the commissioner says,* 'corrupt policemen would know they couldn't get away with their wrong-doing.'

'We can't prosecute without sufficient evidence,' *the DPP says.*

'Then invent it the same as we do,' *the commissioner tells him.*

'These personal recriminations won't solve anything,' *the attorney general says.* 'What's needed is some urgent solution to the crisis these arrests are creating.'

'I'm bound to say that once the papers come to my office,' *the DPP says,* 'I'll have little option but to prosecute. Unless I were to receive a directive from you, Walter.'

'Irreparable damage is being done to the Met,' *the commissioner says.* 'If this goes one step further it will be absolutely disastrous.'

'There is a very serious flaw in the course you suggest, Trevor,' *the attorney general says.* 'Imagine the political consequences if that leaked out. I can't guarantee that it won't, can you?'

'The ground would have to be thoroughly prepared beforehand, so that not to proceed with prosecution would be seen to be in the public interest, Walter,' *the DPP says*. I'm sure our PR people could handle that.'

Sir Walter Pursar thinks about this. 'One would still need to get the Met out of the cleft stick they're in. At the same time satisfy both the media and the officers who have conducted these investigations.'

The attorney general and the DPP exchange looks.

'I'm not going to resign,' *the commissioner says*. 'I don't think it fair that I should be asked to.'

'My dear Denis,' *the AG says expansively*, 'no one's going to ask you to resign. I doubt that would prove sufficiently face-saving anyway.'

'Perhaps if we were to introduce an independent element into the police complaints procedure,' *the DPP suggests*.

'You know what I think about that,' *Whites says*. 'The men in the job won't like it.'

'They should learn to be more prudent,' *the DPP chides*.

'An independent element will look very nice in the window,' *the AG says*. 'But that won't deal with the immediate problem.'

'Well, at our meeting of senior Met officers yesterday morning,' *the commissioner ventures cautiously*, 'Assistant Commissioner Vyvyan made a practical suggestion – one that's absolutely unacceptable, I might add.'

'Vyvyan is one of the main protagonists in this little affair,' *the attorney general says*.

'The evidence against him is quite substantial,' *the DPP says*.

'He strenuously denies absolutely everything,' *the commissioner says*.

'Quite.' *The AG motions the commissioner to continue*. 'What was his proposal?'

'He suggested that rather than simply closing down Bad Apple, the alternative would be to announce a forthcoming date on which the investigation will end. Then in order to facilitate their achieving end date, we bring in officers of the Met to help with inquiries.'

There is a long pause as the AG thinks about this.

'I see,' *he says*.

'It's an absolutely scandalous suggestion,' *the commissioner ventures, testing the water*.

'Who did Vyvyan suggest for inclusion, Sneed, I suppose?' *the AG asks*.

'Well as a matter of fact his name was put forward,' *the commissioner says*. 'Perhaps under the command of Ernie Wiseman. It's absolutely outrageous, of course. but no one would have a better notion of what to steer clear of, if one did want to close this down and save face.'

'The idea being not to prosecute any policemen at all?' *the AG asks*.

'The plan would be to prosecute all those officers charged prior to Sneed's arrest,' *the DPP says*.

'Some three in all,' *the commissioner announces*.

'Three? I see,' *the attorney general says*. 'What do you anticipate Leeper's reaction might be?'

'I think there's a jolly good chance he'll resign from the investigation and go back home,' *Commissioner Whites says*. 'It's ridiculous even thinking like this.' *He chuckles nervously.*

The attorney general considers this. 'I think I would resign in those circumstances.'

The commissioner and the DPP exchange collusive looks.

'I'm not entirely sure Charlie would agree to such a tricky scheme. He's more one for blunt instruments,' *the AG says*.

'He would need to be made fully aware,' *the DPP interjects*, 'that the cabinet couldn't live with the alternative, Walter.'

'I do see that the scheme has a good deal of merit, and could resolve what looks like becoming an intractable problem.' *The AG prods thoughtfully at a golfball with his putting iron.*

'It could solve an absolutely intractable problem,' *the commissioner says*.

'I'll talk to the home secretary,' *the AG says*. 'With a little refining I think that proposition might prove quite acceptable.'

Darkness.

Epilogue

'For those of you who don't know me, I'm Detective Superintendent Sneed,' *Terry Sneed says, addressing an assembly of detectives.* 'For those of you who do know me, you'll know I prefer deeds to words, so I'll be brief. Each of you are part of a team, and as a team we'll get results; results are what everyone wants. You can only function as a team if you know what is going on. It's my intention to keep you informed of what's going on. You're all experienced detectives, you've all had your own individual results and know how they were achieved. I'm not saying those ways are wrong, I'm not saying they are right. But from now on you work as part of this team in my way; that way we'll get a lot more results. Given the open-ended nature of most investigations, a number of you are possibly wondering why at this point it has become necessary to set a completion date on Operation Bad Apple. Especially when its scope and size seemed to grow bigger by the day. It is almost entirely for these reasons that a halt had to be called. The cost was soaring to prohibitive levels; the manpower needed was rendering both the Metropolitan police and the Wiltshire constabulary less effective in fighting crime where it most matters, on the streets. But you have had your successes with three Met officers currently awaiting trial on major corruption charges.' *He pauses briefly.* 'Personally I always subscribed to the one-bad-apple-theory, so I have to admit to being surprised at such widespread corruption. In the past the Met has dealt severely with its wrongdoers, but lately we seem to have become less than scrupulous. Three bad apples, even in a barrel as vast as the Met is a lot. The way in which you've dedicatedly dug them out over the past seventeen months is to your credit. But it hasn't been without its toll: you've worked long, hard hours and have been away from your wives and families for longer than is sometimes good. That has brought its casualties. A much regretted casualty is your assistant chief constable, Alan Leeper, who's had to retire following his stroke – unfortunately we all get old in this job. He was very hard on himself, but he got results. He'll be missed greatly.

'As most of you already know, Acting Chief Constable Bulmer has taken over the investigation with me second in command. But it's no reflection on either of us that Commander Wiseman has taken overall charge of Operation Bad Apple; nor is it any reflection on you that hand-picked Met officers have joined the team. This is to help dig out any more bad apples that might be in our midst. If they're there we want them out.'

He pauses.

'Are there any questions?'